ADHD SUPER-PARENTING
INNOVATIVE AND PRACTICAL TACTICS TO BOOST FOCUS, CONFIDENCE, AND CALM IN YOUR CHAOTIC YET INTELLIGENT SUPER-KID

T.M. ADDWELL

Copyright © 2024 T.M. Addwell. All rights reserved.

The content within this book may not be reproduced, duplicated, or transmitted without direct written permission from the author or the publisher.

Under no circumstances will any blame or legal responsibility be held against the publisher, or author, for any damages, reparation, or monetary loss due to the information contained within this book, either directly or indirectly.

Legal Notice:

This book is copyright protected. It is only for personal use. You cannot amend, distribute, sell, use, quote, or paraphrase any part of the content within this book, without the consent of the author or publisher.

Disclaimer Notice:

Please note the information contained within this document is for educational and entertainment purposes only. All effort has been expended to present accurate, up-to-date, reliable, and complete information. No warranties of any kind are declared or implied. Readers acknowledge that the author is not engaged in the rendering of legal, financial, medical, or professional advice. The content within this book has been derived from various sources. Please consult a licensed professional before attempting any techniques outlined in this book.

By reading this document, the reader agrees that under no circumstances is the author responsible for any losses, direct or indirect, that are incurred as a result of the use of the information contained within this document, including, but not limited to, errors, omissions, or inaccuracies.

TABLE OF CONTENTS

Introduction — 7

1. UNDERSTANDING ADHD IN YOUR CHILD — 11
   What Is ADHD? An In-Depth Look — 11
   Types of ADHD and Their Unique Challenges — 14
   ADHD in Boys versus Girls: Differences and Similarities — 18

2. BUILDING EFFECTIVE ROUTINES AND STRUCTURES — 21
   Developing Morning Routines for Smooth Starts — 21
   Homework Time: Strategies for Focus and Completion — 25
   Bedtime Routines for Better Sleep — 28

3. CREATING A SUPPORTIVE HOME ENVIRONMENT — 33
   Organizing Spaces for ADHD Success — 33
   Reducing Distractions at Home — 37
   Creating Sensory-Friendly Areas — 39

4. EMOTIONAL REGULATION AND SELF-CONTROL — 43
   Stimming — 43
   Mindfulness Practices for ADHD Kids — 48
   Breathing Techniques to Calm Emotional Storms — 51
   Tools for Identifying and Expressing Feelings — 54

5. POSITIVE REINFORCEMENT AND BEHAVIOR MANAGEMENT — 59
   Avoid Medication Until All Other Options Are Exhausted — 59
   Creating Effective Behavior Charts — 62
   Using Positive Reinforcement to Build Good Habits — 65
   Managing Impulsivity: Strategies That Work — 67

6. IMPROVING SOCIAL SKILLS AND
   RELATIONSHIPS   71
   Teaching Social Cues and Body Language   71
   Role-Playing Scenarios to Practice Social Skills   76
   Building and Maintaining Friendships   78

7. COLLABORATING WITH EDUCATORS AND
   SCHOOLS   81
   Advocating for IEPs and 504 Plans   81
   Building Strong Relationships with Teachers   85
   Strategies for Successful Parent-Teacher Meetings   88

8. ADDRESSING COMMON CHALLENGES AT
   SCHOOL   95
   Strategies for Focus and Attention in the
   Classroom   95
   Homework Help: Making After-School Time
   Productive   99
   Handling Bullying and Social Issues at School   101

9. HOLISTIC APPROACHES TO ADHD
   MANAGEMENT   105
   Nutrition and ADHD: Foods That Help   105
   Exercise Routines to Boost Focus and Energy   109
   Sleep Hygiene: Ensuring Restful Nights   111

10. EMPOWERING YOUR ADHD CHILD   115
    Discovering and Nurturing Your Child's Strengths   115
    Success Stories: Inspiring Examples of ADHD
    Brilliance   118
    Building Self-Esteem and Confidence   121

11. NAVIGATING PUBLIC SPACES AND SOCIAL
    SITUATIONS   125
    Preparing for Outings: What to Pack and Plan   125
    Handling Meltdowns in Public   128
    Navigating Social Gatherings and Events   130

12. SELF-CARE FOR PARENTS   133
    Stress Management Techniques for Parents   133
    Building Your Support Network   137
    Finding Time for Self-Care Amid the Chaos   142

13. BUILDING A SUPPORTIVE COMMUNITY ... 145
    Joining Local and Online Support Groups ... 145
    Engaging with Community Resources ... 148
    Creating a Supportive Family Network ... 151

14. LONG-TERM STRATEGIES FOR SUCCESS ... 155
    Transitioning to Adolescence: New Challenges and Solutions ... 155
    Preparing for Independence: Life Skills for ADHD Teens ... 158
    Maintaining Progress: Consistency and Adaptation ... 160
    Celebrating Milestones: Recognizing Achievements Along the Way ... 162

    Conclusion ... 167
    References ... 171

INTRODUCTION

Let's not beat around the bush; raising a child with ADHD will be a monumental challenge, but it will also be extremely rewarding. We see the spark in their eyes, the creativity in their souls, and the rambunctious energy that drives them. Yet, we also face the whirlwind of chaos, the frustrations of unmet expectations, and the exhaustion that often accompanies daily struggles. You are not alone. I am T.M. Addwell, an everyday father who is walking this path with you. Not only am I raising a child with ADHD, but I, too, have been diagnosed with ADHD. I know the trials and tribulations that come with our unique and often frustrating "superpower."

This book, *ADHD Super-Parenting: Innovative and Practical Tactics to Boost Focus, Confidence, and Calm in Your Chaotic yet Intelligent Super-Kid*. is born out of my mission to find great resources and practical tactics to simplify and stabilize family life and ensure our children thrive—socially, academically, and within the family unit. This journey has not been easy, but it has been enlightening. I have gathered research-based strategies that can stabilize our family lives and ensure our parental sanity.

The purpose of this book is clear—to provide a thorough, research-based parenting guide for parents of children with ADHD. We will explore practical tactics that can improve your parenting experience and enhance the home life of families with ADHD children. Along the way, I want you to feel heard and sympathized with. I get it because I'm here in the weeds with you. Parenting a neurodivergent child requires not just knowledge but also empathy and self-care.

My vision for this book is to uncover and share the rich tapestry of strategies and insights that have shaped my understanding of ADHD. The inspiration behind the title is simple: our children are super-kids, and we, as parents, have the power to guide them to booming success. This book is a roadmap for that journey, filled with practical advice and heartfelt support.

This book is for parents like you—parents looking for ways to connect with their ADHD children, parents who want to create a stable and nurturing environment, and parents who need to care for themselves while caring for their children. Whether you are new to this journey, have been on it for years, or are just looking for general parenting tips, there is something here for you.

Understanding ADHD in its cultural and social context is crucial. ADHD is not just a medical condition but a way of experiencing the world around us. Our children will not be defined by their diagnosis but by their unique strengths and challenges. We must approach this journey with openness, compassion, and, most of all, patience. Recognizing the educational value of these strategies can empower us to support our children in meaningful and effective ways.

Let me share a bit about my background. As a father of a child with ADHD, I have faced many of the same challenges you face. My personal experience, combined with my own ADHD, has driven me to seek out the best resources and strategies. This book is a culmination of that search. I have drawn from significant studies on children with ADHD conducted over the past twenty years, ensuring the information is current, reliable, and relevant. I have felt the frustration you feel.

This book's structure is simple and user-friendly. Each chapter focuses on a different area of parenting a child with ADHD. We will cover various topics, from creating routines and managing behavior to fostering emotional resilience and supporting academic success. Each chapter presents practical tactics that you can implement right away. Some tactics may be familiar, while others may offer new insights. This balance ensures that there is something for everyone.

The research methodology behind this book is thorough. I have relied on primary sources, including academic papers, expert interviews, and real-life experiences from parents like you and me. This blend of sources adds depth and authenticity to the strategies presented. You will find that each tactic is backed by research and tested in real-world scenarios. My heaviest influence on the data and techniques described in this book came from A. Mehrabian, a gentleman who has pioneered studies on child language skills, non-verbal communication, and the effects of video games and screen time on children.

You will notice a supportive and empathetic tone as you read this book. Parenting, in general, is a monumental undertaking; adding another variable, such as ADHD, increases the difficulty level. I aim to make the content engaging and accessible. You will find a mix of simple and advanced vocabulary, ensuring the information is easy to understand yet stimulating. My goal is to keep you engaged while providing valuable insights and easy-to-implement strategies.

The book includes visual aids and interactive elements to enhance your experience. You will find chart ideas, checklists, and real-life examples that bring the strategies to life. These features make the book more dynamic and engaging, helping you apply the tactics in your daily life.

So, dear parents, I invite you to join me on this journey. Together, we will explore practical and effective tactics to guide your superkid. We will add stability to your family life and success to your child's academic life. The path may be challenging but filled with joy and triumph. Let us embrace this adventure and empower our children to thrive.

UNDERSTANDING ADHD IN YOUR CHILD

We were in the hobby store for the first time, and I noticed something different about my oldest child's behavior. She couldn't stay still for more than a few seconds, darting from aisle to aisle, touching everything in sight. Her boundless energy was both fascinating and exhausting. I remember wondering if it was just the usual childhood exuberance or something more. This question is one many parents of ADHD children grapple with daily. Understanding ADHD in your child is the cornerstone of effective parenting strategies. It allows you to see beyond the challenges and recognize your child's unique strengths and capabilities.

WHAT IS ADHD? AN IN-DEPTH LOOK

Attention Deficit Hyperactivity Disorder, commonly known as ADHD, is a neurodevelopmental disorder that affects both cognitive and behavioral functioning. The condition is characterized by persistent patterns of inattention, hyperactivity, and impulsivity, which can significantly impact daily activities and interpersonal relationships. ADHD is more than just an issue of being overly active or inattentive; it involves a complex interplay of brain function and environmental factors. Historically, ADHD was often misunderstood and misdiagnosed, labeled as mere "bad behavior" or "lack of discipline." Today, we understand that ADHD stems from the brain's unique wiring, affecting executive functions such as organizing, planning, and regulating emotions.

The evolution of ADHD understanding has been fascinating. In the early twentieth century, ADHD was often referred to as "minimal brain dysfunction," a term that failed to capture the condition's complexity. It wasn't until the late twentieth century that ADHD became widely recognized as a legitimate medical diagnosis. Advances in neuroimaging and genetic studies have since deepened our understanding, revealing that ADHD is linked to differences in brain structure and function. This historical context underscores the importance of ongoing research and education in refining our approach to ADHD.

The core symptoms of ADHD are typically categorized into three main areas: inattention, hyperactivity, and impulsivity. Inattention involves difficulties sustaining focus, following through on tasks, and organizing activities. Children with inattention may often make careless mistakes, lose things necessary for tasks, or seem not to listen when spoken to directly. Hyperactivity includes excessive fidgeting, an inability to stay seated, and a tendency to run or climb in inappropriate situations. This constant motion can be particularly challenging in structured environments like classrooms. Impulsivity manifests as interrupting others, difficulty waiting for one's turn, and acting without considering the consequences. These symptoms can vary widely in severity and presentation, making each child's experience with ADHD unique.

Diagnosing ADHD involves a comprehensive evaluation process. The DSM-5, the Diagnostic and Statistical Manual of Mental Disorders, outlines specific criteria for diagnosing ADHD. These criteria include a persistent pattern of inattention and/or hyperactivity-impulsivity that interferes with functioning or development. Symptoms must be present before age twelve and occur in two or more settings, such as home and school. Additionally, the symptoms should not be better explained by another diagnosis. Professional diagnosis typically involves behavioral assessments, parent and teacher questionnaires, and sometimes interviews with the child. This thorough process helps avoid misdiagnosis and ensures that children receive the appropriate support and interventions.

Diagnostic Tools: Behavioral Assessments and Questionnaires

Behavioral assessments and questionnaires are crucial tools in diagnosing ADHD. These tools gather comprehensive information about a child's behaviors across different settings. Parents and teachers often complete standardized questionnaires that rate the child's behavior, providing valuable insights into patterns, ADHD types, and their triggers. Behavioral assessments may include direct observations and structured tasks to evaluate attention, impulse control, and executive functioning. ADHD shares symptoms with other conditions, such as anxiety and learning disabilities. A thorough evaluation helps differentiate ADHD from these conditions, ensuring that children receive the most effective interventions.

ADHD is a common condition affecting millions of children worldwide. According to the Centers for Disease Control and Prevention (CDC), approximately 6.1 million children in the United States have been diagnosed with ADHD. This prevalence highlights the need for awareness and resources to support affected families. ADHD occurs across all demographics, but specific patterns emerge. Boys are more frequently diagnosed with ADHD than girls, possibly due to differences in symptom presentation and diagnostic biases. ADHD can affect children from all socio-economic backgrounds, though access to diagnosis and treatment may vary. Understanding these prevalence rates and demographic patterns underscores the importance of advocating for equitable access to ADHD resources and support.

Inattention, hyperactivity, and impulsivity may manifest differently depending on the child. For instance, a child struggling with inattention will frequently lose school supplies, forget instructions, or daydream excessively. On the other hand, a child dealing with hyperactivity may be constantly on the go and unable to sit still during meals or class activities. Impulsivity could lead to interrupting conversations or taking unnecessary risks without considering the potential consequences. Recognizing these symptoms is the first step toward seeking professional help and implementing effective strategies to support your child.

Understanding ADHD involves more than just recognizing symptoms; it requires a comprehensive approach, considering the child's environment, experiences, and individual strengths. By gaining a more profound understanding of ADHD, you can better support your child and create a nurturing environment that fosters their growth and development. This chapter aims to provide you with the knowledge and tools to navigate the complexities of ADHD, ensuring that your child can thrive.

TYPES OF ADHD AND THEIR UNIQUE CHALLENGES

Navigating the world of ADHD is complex, especially when you consider the different ways it can manifest in children. ADHD is not a one-size-fits-all diagnosis; it comes in three main types, each with its own set of behaviors and challenges. The first type, predominantly inattentive presentation, is characterized mainly by issues with attention and focus. Children with this type may seem forgetful, easily distracted, and disorganized. Imagine a child who frequently and easily gets sidetracked or cannot focus enough to complete simple tasks. These children may not disrupt the classroom, but their academic performance can suffer due to missed details and incomplete assignments.

The second type is predominantly hyperactive-impulsive presentation. Children of this type are often in constant motion and unable to sit still for long periods. They may fidget excessively, have trouble playing quietly, and frequently act without thinking. Picture a child who can't stay seated during meals, constantly interrupts others, or takes unnecessary risks. Their boundless energy and impulsive actions can be disruptive, making it difficult for them to thrive in structured environments like school or social gatherings.

The third type is combined presentation, where symptoms of inattention and hyperactivity-impulsivity are present. These children face the dual challenge of managing two sets of symptoms, which can make daily life particularly overwhelming. They may struggle with organization and focus while also dealing with constant motion and impulsive behaviors. Imagine a child who forgets their school assignments and disrupts the class with their inability to stay seated. This combination can make it challenging to implement effective strategies, as you need to address both aspects simultaneously.

Each type of ADHD presents unique challenges that can affect various aspects of a child's life. For children with predominantly inattentive presentations, missed details and disorganization can lead to poor academic performance and frustration. These children may be perceived as lazy or uninterested, affecting their self-esteem. In a classroom setting, they will need help to follow instructions or stay on task, leading to incomplete work and lower grades. Socially, they may find it challenging to keep up with conversations or remember important details about their friends, which can impact their relationships.

Children with predominantly hyperactive-impulsive presentations face different hurdles. Their constant motion and impulsive actions can be disruptive, leading to disciplinary issues at school. Teachers find it challenging to manage their behavior, and peers may avoid them due to their disruptive actions. This can lead to social isolation and feelings of rejection. At home, these children may have difficulty following rules and routines, creating a chaotic environment that can be stressful for the entire family.

For children with combined presentation, the challenges are compounded. They must navigate the difficulties of both inattentive and hyperactive-impulsive symptoms. This combination can make school particularly challenging, as they need help to focus on their work while constantly being on the move. Social interactions can be equally tricky, as their impulsive behaviors may alienate peers, and their inattentiveness may cause them to miss social cues. Managing dual symptom sets requires a nuanced approach that addresses both aspects of ADHD.

Recognizing the type of ADHD your child has is crucial for tailoring effective strategies. Focus techniques and organizational aids can benefit children with predominantly inattentive presentations. Visual schedules, checklists, and timers can help them stay on task and manage their responsibilities. For instance, setting a timer for homework sessions can provide a clear structure, while visual schedules remind them of their daily tasks. Incorporating frequent breaks can also improve focus and reduce frustration.

For those with predominantly hyperactive-impulsive presentations, physical activities and impulse control methods are essential. Encouraging regular physical exercise can help channel their energy positively. Activities like sports or dance can provide an outlet for their restlessness. It can also be beneficial to implement impulse control techniques, such as teaching them to stop and think before acting. Simple strategies like using a stress ball or practicing deep breathing can help manage their impulsivity.

Children with combined presentation require an integrated approach that addresses both inattentiveness and hyperactivity-impulsivity. Combining focus techniques with physical activities can create a balanced routine. For example, starting the day with physical activity can help manage their energy levels, followed by structured tasks with clear breaks in between. Combining visual aids, timers, and relaxation techniques can provide a comprehensive strategy to manage their symptoms.

Consider the case of a child with predominantly inattentive presentation. This child might struggle in school, often missing instructions or forgetting to turn in homework. A parent could implement a visual schedule and dedicated homework time with frequent breaks, helping the child stay organized and focused. On the other hand, a child with predominantly hyperactive-impulsive presentation will be constantly on the move, disrupting class and social settings. Encouraging this child to participate in sports like soccer or basketball can help manage their energy levels. Additionally, teaching impulse control techniques, such as counting to ten before speaking, can improve their interactions.

In the classroom, managing a hyperactive-impulsive child can be challenging. Teachers might find it helpful to provide this child with a sensory toy or allow short, supervised breaks to move around. These tactics can help reduce disruptions while allowing the child to manage their restlessness.

Navigating the intricacies of ADHD requires a tailored approach that considers each type's unique challenges and strengths. Understanding these distinctions is the first step in providing the support your child needs to thrive.

ADHD IN BOYS VERSUS GIRLS: DIFFERENCES AND SIMILARITIES

ADHD is more frequently diagnosed in boys than in girls. According to the CDC, boys are about three times more likely to be diagnosed with ADHD than girls. This significant difference in diagnosis rates can be attributed to several factors, including diagnostic biases and how symptoms manifest differently between boys and girls. Boys often display more overt symptoms, such as hyperactivity and impulsivity, which are easily noticeable. In contrast, girls may exhibit more subtle signs of inattention, which can be overlooked or misinterpreted as daydreaming or shyness.

The disparity in diagnosis rates is not just a matter of statistics; it has real-world implications. Boys exhibiting hyperactive behaviors are more likely to draw attention from teachers and parents, leading to earlier and more frequent diagnoses. Girls, on the other hand, may be quietly struggling with inattention, often going unnoticed. This diagnostic bias means that many girls with ADHD do not receive the support they need, leading to academic and social challenges that persist into adulthood. Girls may also be more prone to anxiety and depression, conditions that can mask or overshadow ADHD symptoms.

The challenges specific to girls with ADHD are significant. Underdiagnosis is a major issue, as the subtlety of their symptoms often leads to them being overlooked. This lack of recognition means that girls are less likely to receive early interventions, which are crucial for managing ADHD effectively. Social pressures also play a role in the difficulties faced by girls with ADHD. They may feel the need to conform to societal expectations of being well-behaved and attentive, leading to internalized stress and anxiety. Peer relationships can be particularly challenging, as subtle social cues and the dynamics of friendships may be harder for them to navigate.

Girls with ADHD are also more likely to face comorbid conditions such as anxiety and depression. These conditions can exacerbate the difficulties associated with ADHD, creating a cycle of emotional and behavioral challenges. The presence of comorbid conditions often complicates the diagnosis and treatment of ADHD, as the symptoms can overlap and interact in complex ways. For example, a girl struggling with both ADHD and anxiety may find it even harder to focus in school as her anxiety heightens her inattention.

Recognizing ADHD in girls requires a keen eye and understanding of the subtleties involved. Parents should look for signs such as subtle inattention, social withdrawal, and a tendency to be easily overwhelmed by tasks. Girls may also exhibit perfectionistic tendencies as they try to compensate for their difficulties by striving to meet high standards. It is essential to pay attention to these signs and seek a professional evaluation if ADHD is suspected. Early recognition and intervention can prevent many of the academic and social difficulties that girls with ADHD face.

The importance of early intervention cannot be overstated. When ADHD is identified early, parents and educators can implement strategies to support the child's development. These strategies may include individualized education plans, behavioral therapy, and social skills training. Early intervention helps build a strong foundation, enabling girls with ADHD to navigate their challenges more effectively and develop their strengths.

Understanding the differences and similarities in how ADHD manifests in boys and girls can help us better support our children. Boys may need more strategies to manage hyperactivity and impulsivity, while girls may benefit from interventions that address inattention and emotional regulation. This is not to say boys can't suffer from inattention and anxiety and girls can't suffer from hyperactivity and impulsivity: they certainly can. Children with ADHD possess unique strengths, and recognizing these can help them thrive. By tailoring our approaches to meet their needs, we can create a more supportive and nurturing environment for all children.

In the following chapters, we will explore practical tactics and strategies tailored to the needs of children with ADHD. From building effective routines and creating supportive home environments to fostering emotional regulation and improving social skills, this book provides the tools and insights to guide your super-kid to success. Understanding the nuances of ADHD in different kids is just the beginning. Together, we will navigate the complexities of ADHD, focusing on actionable steps that can make a meaningful difference in your child's life.

BUILDING EFFECTIVE ROUTINES AND STRUCTURES

Imagine trying to build a house with no blueprint. Daily, you make decisions on the fly, improvising as you go. The result is chaos, with no apparent structure or stability. This analogy is like parenting a child with ADHD without established routines and structures. Building effective routines is like creating a blueprint for your days, offering a sense of predictability and calm in an otherwise turbulent environment. For children with ADHD, routines are not just helpful—they're transformative. They provide the framework that helps these children navigate their days with confidence and focus.

DEVELOPING MORNING ROUTINES FOR SMOOTH STARTS

Mornings can set the tone for the entire day. For a child with ADHD, a chaotic morning can lead to a day filled with anxiety and frustration. A consistent morning routine can make a world of difference. Predictable mornings reduce stress and help children know what to expect, which is particularly important for those who struggle with transitions and unpredictability. When children start their day positively, they are more likely to remain focused and ready to tackle the day's challenges. Consistent routines also provide security, making it easier for children to manage their emotions and behaviors.

To set up a successful morning routine, establish a consistent wake-up time. This regularity helps regulate the body's internal clock, making it easier for your child to wake up feeling refreshed. Once your child is awake, guide them through morning hygiene tasks like dressing, brushing their teeth, and washing their face. These tasks might seem mundane, but they are essential for preparing your child for the day ahead. Consider using visual aids like picture charts for younger children or written checklists for older children to help them stay on track. Visual schedules can be particularly effective, providing a precise sequence of tasks that your child can follow independently.

Breakfast is another essential element of a successful morning routine. Opt for nutritious and quick meal ideas that provide sustained energy and focus. Foods rich in protein, such as eggs or yogurt, combined with whole grains and fruits, can stabilize blood sugar levels and prevent mid-morning crashes. Preparing backpacks and supplies the night before can also streamline the morning process, reducing last-minute scrambles. Encourage your child to lay out their clothes and pack their school bag before bed. This practice saves time and empowers your child to take responsibility for their readiness.

Visual aids and checklists can significantly enhance the effectiveness of your morning routine. Visual schedules, such as picture charts, can be advantageous for younger children who benefit from visual cues. These charts can depict each step of the morning routine, from waking up to heading out the door. Written checklists can be a practical tool for older children to ensure they complete each task. Reward systems can provide additional motivation. You can create a simple reward chart where your child earns a star or sticker for each completed task. Accumulating a certain number of stars can lead to a reward, such as extra screen time or a small treat.

Mornings present a unique set of challenges, especially for children with ADHD. Difficulty waking up, slow transitions, and resistance to morning tasks are common hurdles. Consider using an alarm clock with gradual light to help your child wake up more naturally. These clocks simulate a sunrise, gently increasing light intensity to ease your child into wakefulness. Setting time limits for each task can also be effective. Use timers to allocate specific durations for tasks like brushing teeth or getting dressed. This approach helps your child stay focused and creates a sense of urgency without overwhelming them.

Encouraging independence is another important aspect of developing a successful morning routine. Gradually increase your child's responsibility by allowing them to take charge of specific tasks. Start with simple steps, like choosing their clothes or setting their own alarm. As they become more comfortable, consider introducing more complex tasks, such as preparing their breakfast or packing their school bag. This gradual increase in responsibility builds their confidence and fosters a sense of accomplishment.

Morning Routine Visual Schedule

Creating a morning routine visual schedule can be a game-changer for you and your child. Here's a simple way to set it up:

1. **Wake-Up Time**

   - **Visual Aid:** Picture of a child waking up
   - **Task:** Set a consistent alarm

2. **Morning Hygiene**

   - **Visual Aid:** Picture of brushing teeth and washing face
   - **Task:** Complete hygiene tasks

3. **Breakfast**

   - **Visual Aid:** Picture of a healthy breakfast
   - **Task:** Eat a nutritious meal

4. **Packing for School**

   - **Visual Aid:** Picture of a packed backpack
   - **Task:** Prepare backpacks and supplies
   - **Fun Game or Activity (avoid screen time)**
   - **Visual Aid:** Picture of kids playing a board or card game
   - **Task:** Sight words, spelling test practice, memory or matching games, quick-fire math problems: *anything* to **stimulate** that brain and knock the remaining fog off.

   Check out the charts I designed and use myself at https://charts4kids.printify.me/

Place the visual aid in a common area, such as the kitchen or bathroom, where your child can easily see it. Encourage them to check off each task as they complete it, providing a sense of accomplishment and structure.

Implementing these strategies can transform your mornings from chaotic to calm. By establishing a consistent routine, using visual aids, and encouraging independence, you can help your child start their day with confidence and focus. These small steps can significantly improve your child's ability to manage their ADHD symptoms and navigate their daily activities successfully.

HOMEWORK TIME: STRATEGIES FOR FOCUS AND COMPLETION

Creating a designated homework space can significantly affect how effectively your child completes their assignments. This space should be quiet and organized, free from distractions that pull their attention from the task. Think of a corner in your home with low noise levels, away from the hustle and bustle of daily activities. Ensure this space is well-lit and stocked with all the necessary supplies like pencils, paper, and a calculator. Keeping these items within reach reduces the need for your child to get up and search for materials, which can easily lead to distractions.

Establishing a homework schedule is another critical component. Setting a regular homework time that aligns with your child's natural energy levels and the family's overall schedule can help create a manageable routine. Consistent timing is vital. Aim to have your child start their homework at a similar time each day. This consistency helps their body and mind get into a rhythm, making it easier to transition into work mode. Incorporate scheduled breaks into this time. Short intervals of rest can refresh your child and help maintain their focus. Balancing homework with extracurricular activities is also essential. Ensure your child has time for obligations and relaxation, ensuring that neither necessity is neglected.

Techniques to enhance focus and motivation can transform homework time from a dreaded task into a more manageable one. One effective method is the Pomodoro Technique, which involves working in short, focused bursts followed by brief breaks. For example, have your child work for ten minutes and then take a five-minute break. This approach can make the workload feel less overwhelming and helps maintain their focus. Positive reinforcement is another powerful tool. Rewarding your child for completing tasks can boost their motivation. These rewards don't have to be extravagant. Simple incentives, like extra screen time or a small treat, can be very effective. Parental involvement also plays a crucial role. Sitting with your child, offering support and encouragement, can make them feel more confident and less isolated in their efforts.

Managing homework-related stress is equally important. Homework can often be a source of anxiety, especially for children with ADHD. One way to reduce this stress is through relaxation techniques. Encourage your child to practice deep breathing exercises before starting their homework. These techniques can help calm their mind and body, making focusing easier. Encouraging self-advocacy is another essential strategy. Teach your child to communicate their needs and challenges to their teachers. Effective communication can help you get the necessary accommodations and support. Open communication with teachers is critical. Regularly discussing your child's workload and difficulties can help address issues before they become overwhelming.

Homework Schedule Planner

Creating a homework schedule planner can be an effective way to keep your child on track. Here's a simple template to get you started:

1. **Homework Time**

    - **Start Time:** 4:00 PM
    - **End Time:** 5:30 PM

2. **Breaks**

    - **First Break:** 4:25 PM - 4:30 PM (I've found this to be the perfect time to make a healthy afternoon snack)
    - **Second Break:** 4:55 PM - 5:00 PM

3. **Tasks**

    - **Math Homework:** 4:00 PM - 4:25 PM
    - **Break:** 4:25 PM - 4:30 PM
    - **Reading Assignment:** 4:30 PM - 4:55 PM
    - **Break:** 4:55 PM - 5:00 PM
    - **STEM Project:** 5:00 PM - 5:30 PM

4. **Rewards**

    - **Completion Reward:** 15 minutes of extra screen time, extra dessert, more outside time before shower time, etc.

This planner helps break down homework time into manageable chunks, incorporating breaks and rewards to keep your child motivated and focused. Place it in a visible spot, like above the homework desk, where your child can easily refer to it.

Creating a designated homework space and establishing a consistent schedule are foundational steps in managing homework time. These efforts, combined with techniques to enhance focus and strategies to reduce stress, can make homework less daunting and more productive. Each child is unique, so feel free to adjust these suggestions to fit your child's specific needs and preferences.

BEDTIME ROUTINES FOR BETTER SLEEP

A consistent bedtime routine is a cornerstone for children with ADHD. Quality sleep directly impacts their focus, behavior, and overall well-being. Studies have shown that children who adhere to a regular sleep schedule perform better academically and exhibit fewer behavioral issues. Predictability at bedtime provides security and reduces anxiety, making it easier for children to wind down and transition to sleep. For a child with ADHD, this predictability can be a game-changer, helping them to manage the chaos that often fills their minds.

To establish an effective bedtime routine, start with wind-down activities that signal the end of the day. Reading a book or engaging in quiet play can reduce stimulation and prepare the mind for rest. These activities should be calming and enjoyable, setting a positive tone for bedtime. Following these activities with hygiene tasks like bathing and brushing teeth can create a seamless transition to bed. These tasks promote good health and are consistent markers in the bedtime routine. Setting a bedtime and sticking to it every night helps regulate your child's internal clock, making it easier for them to fall asleep and wake up at the exact same time each day.

Creating a calming environment is crucial. Dim the lights and play soft music to signal it's time to relax. The bedroom should be a sanctuary of calm, free from distractions like electronic devices. Consider using blackout curtains to block light and a white noise machine to drown out disruptive sounds. These minor adjustments can make a significant difference in creating a peaceful atmosphere conducive to sleep.

Using visual aids and timers can also be beneficial. A visual bedtime schedule with pictures or written steps can guide your child through each part of the routine. For instance, a chart that shows a picture of a child brushing their teeth followed by one reading a book can provide clear, visual instructions. Timers can help allocate specific durations of time for each bedtime task, ensuring the routine flows smoothly and doesn't drag on. Establishing a reading habit with bedtime stories can be a comforting and enjoyable way to end the day, fostering a love for reading and helping your child wind down.

Addressing common bedtime challenges is essential for maintaining a successful routine. Children with ADHD often have difficulty winding down, resistance to sleep, and may experience nighttime awakenings. Calming techniques like deep breathing and progressive muscle relaxation can help ease your child into sleep. Teach your child to take slow, deep breaths or to tense and relax different muscle groups. These techniques can help reduce physical tension and calm the mind. Setting and enforcing bedtime boundaries is equally important. Make it clear that bedtime is non-negotiable and stick to the established routine. Consistency is critical in helping your child understand and adhere to the routine.

Nighttime comfort items can also help ease your child into sleep. Security blankets, stuffed animals, or even a favorite pillow can provide a sense of comfort and security. These items can help your child feel safe and relaxed, making it easier for them to drift off to sleep. If your child experiences nighttime awakenings, gently guide them back to bed and encourage them to use the same calming techniques to fall back asleep.

Bedtime Routine Visual Schedule

Creating a bedtime routine visual schedule can help your child transition smoothly through bedtime tasks. Here's a simple example:

1. **Wind-Down Activities**

   - **Visual Aid:** Picture of a child reading a book
   - **Task:** Read for 15 minutes

2. **Hygiene**

   - **Visual Aid:** Picture of brushing teeth
   - **Task:** Brush teeth and wash face

3. **Setting a Bedtime**

   - **Visual Aid:** Picture of a kid in bed
   - **Task:** Go to bed at 9:00 PM

4. **Creating a Calming Environment**

   - **Visual Aid:** Picture of a dimly lit room
   - **Task:** Dim lights and play soft music

This visual schedule can be placed in your child's bedroom or bathroom, where they can easily see it. Encourage them to follow each step and check off tasks as they complete them, providing a sense of accomplishment and routine.

Developing a consistent bedtime routine is vital. By incorporating calming activities, setting a specific bedtime, creating a soothing environment, and using visual aids, you can help your child transition smoothly into sleep. Addressing common bedtime challenges with calming techniques and providing comfort items can further enhance the effectiveness of the routine. These small steps can significantly improve your child's sleep quality, focus, and overall well-being.

Building effective routines and structures goes beyond just bedtime. The next chapter will explore creating a supportive home environment that fosters growth and stability for your ADHD child. From organizing spaces to reducing distractions and creating sensory-friendly areas, we will delve into practical strategies to transform your home into a nurturing and empowering space.

CREATING A SUPPORTIVE HOME ENVIRONMENT

Imagine your home as a sanctuary where each corner is thoughtfully designed to cater to the unique needs of your child. The right environment can make a world of difference, transforming chaotic moments into manageable routines and fostering a sense of calm and stability. Creating a supportive home environment is not just about organization; it's about setting up spaces that promote focus, creativity, and relaxation. It is about understanding that your child's environment can amplify their challenges or be a powerful tool to help them succeed.

ORGANIZING SPACES FOR ADHD SUCCESS

Designating specific areas for different activities is important. These children often struggle with transitions and need clear cues to understand what is expected of them. Having designated spaces for activities like homework, play, and relaxation can help them know where to focus their energy and what behavior is appropriate in each area. For instance, a quiet, well-lit homework station equipped with all necessary supplies can minimize distractions and make it easier for your child to concentrate on their tasks. This area should be free from non-essential items and designed to be inviting yet functional. A dedicated desk, comfortable chair, and ample lighting can create an environment conducive to learning.

In contrast, a play area should allow your child to let their energy and creativity flow freely. This space should be safe and stocked with toys, art supplies, and other items encouraging physical activity and imaginative play. A well-organized play area can help channel your child's energy positively, reducing the likelihood of disruptive behavior. Establishing boundaries within this space is essential, making it clear that this is where they can engage in more active and noisy activities.

Equally important is a relaxation corner, a comfortable space filled with calming items where your child can retreat when they need to unwind. This area could include soft cushions, a cozy blanket, and a few favorite books or quiet toys. Creating a sensory-friendly space with soft lighting and soothing textures can help your child self-regulate when overwhelmed. This corner can serve as a haven where your child knows they can go to relax and recharge.

Using organizational tools and aids can help keep these spaces organized and clutter-free, which is important for minimizing distractions. Labeling systems with clear labels for bins and shelves can make it easier for your child to find and put away items, fostering independence and responsibility. Color-coded folders and bins can be particularly effective for organizing school supplies and toys. For instance, using a different color for each subject can help your child keep their schoolwork organized and reduce the stress of finding materials. Visual schedules displaying daily routines and tasks can also provide structure and consistency, allowing your child to know what to expect and when.

Creating a clutter-free environment is essential for helping children with ADHD focus better. Clutter can be overwhelming and distracting, making it difficult for your child to concentrate on their tasks. Regular decluttering sessions, whether weekly or monthly, help maintain a tidy and organized space. A minimalist approach, where only necessary items are found in each space, can further reduce distractions. This approach involves keeping surfaces clear and storing items out of sight when they are not in use.

Involving your child in the organizing process is another critical element. This involvement fosters a sense of ownership and responsibility, making them more likely to maintain the organization. Let your child choose organizational tools like bins or folders, allowing them to have a say in arranging their space. This choice can make them feel more invested in keeping the area tidy. Collaboratively arranging items and furniture can also be a bonding experience, allowing you to teach your child valuable organizational skills. Using the mantra "Don't put it down, put it away" can help reinforce the habit of immediate organization, reducing the likelihood of clutter accumulating.

Interactive Element: Organizing Checklist

Creating an organizing checklist can be a practical tool for maintaining a tidy environment. Here's an example:

1. **Homework Station**

   - **Clear Desk:** Remove non-essential items
   - **Organize Supplies:** Use labeled bins and color-coded folders
   - **Check Lighting:** Ensure the area is well-lit

2. **Play Area**

   - **Toy Storage:** Use clear bins with labels
   - **Art Supplies:** Keep organized in a caddy
   - **Safety Check:** Ensure the area is safe for active play

3. **Relaxation Corner**

   - **Comfort Items:** Arrange cushions and blankets
   - **Calming Tools:** Include soft lighting and soothing textures
   - **Quiet Toys:** Keep a selection of quiet, favorite toys

Post the checklist in a common area and use it during regular decluttering sessions to ensure that each space remains organized and functional.

Designating specific areas for activities, using organizational tools, maintaining a clutter-free environment, and involving your child in the organizing process can transform your home into a supportive environment. These strategies provide structure and predictability, helping your child navigate their daily activities more quickly and confidently.

REDUCING DISTRACTIONS AT HOME

A calm, focused environment is of paramount importance for a child with ADHD. Common distractions can quickly derail their concentration and make daily tasks more challenging. Noise is a significant distraction. Background TV, loud conversations, and even household appliances can create a cacophony that muddles their ability to focus. Visual clutter—overstimulating decorations, messy rooms, and disorganized spaces—adds to the chaos, making it difficult for your child to settle into a task. Technology presents another layer of distraction. Unrestricted screen time and easy access to devices can pull your child into a vortex of stimulation, making it hard for them to transition back to human interaction or other activities.

Implementing noise reduction strategies can help create a quieter home environment that supports focus. White noise machines are an effective tool. They drown out background noise, creating a steady, soothing sound to help your child concentrate. Designate quiet zones in your home, areas where silent activities are encouraged. These can be places where your child goes to read, draw, or complete homework. Soundproofing techniques, such as rugs, curtains, and door seals, can reduce noise. Soft materials absorb sound, preventing it from bouncing around the room and creating an echo. These small changes can significantly reduce auditory distractions, making it easier for your child to focus.

Managing technology use is also crucial. Screen time schedules can allocate specific times for device use, ensuring that technology supports rather than hinders focus. If possible, you can have a rule that screens are only allowed after homework is completed. Educational apps can be a beneficial tool, providing interactive learning experiences that engage your child's mind in productive ways. Establish device-free zones, areas in your home where technology is not allowed. These can be spaces designated for family time, meals, or relaxation. Using devices collaboratively can also help. Playing video games or watching hobby or nature videos together can make the transition to other tasks more natural. Children often prefer to engage in these activities with a parent, which can create opportunities for bonding and make it easier to move on to other, non-screen-based activities.

Creating visually calming spaces can also make a big difference. Neutral color palettes can create a serene environment using calming colors in the decor. Soft blues, greens, and earth tones are particularly effective. Simple, clean lines should be favored over overly complex patterns and decorations. Avoid collages and "high-volume" decorations in your child's calm space. An organized storage solution is vital to keeping items out of sight. Use storage bins, shelves, and cabinets to keep toys, books, and other items neatly stored away when unused.

Regular decluttering sessions can help maintain this order. Depending on your family's needs, these sessions can be weekly or monthly. During these times, involve your child in the process, teaching them the importance of tidying their environment. A minimalist approach, where only necessary items are kept in each space, can reduce visual clutter and make it easier for your child to focus. This approach involves regularly assessing which items are genuinely needed and removing anything contributing to clutter.

Noise Reduction Tools

Managing noise effectively can transform your home environment. Consider these tools:

1. **White Noise Machine:** Creates a steady background sound
2. **Rugs and Curtains:** Absorb sound and reduce echo
3. **Door Seals:** Prevent noise from entering rooms
4. **Partitions**: Block noise and visual stimuli happening in adjacent areas
5. **Acoustic paneling**: Reduces reverberation and reduces overall noise

Use these tools in various parts of your home to create quieter, more focused spaces for your child.

In summary, reducing distractions at home involves addressing noise, visual clutter, and technology use. Implementing noise reduction strategies, managing technology, and creating visually calming spaces can significantly improve your child's ability to focus. These changes, though small, can make a substantial impact on your child's daily life, providing them with the environment they need to thrive.

CREATING SENSORY-FRIENDLY AREAS

Understanding sensory needs is critical when raising a child with ADHD. Sensory processing refers to how the nervous system receives messages from the senses and turns them into appropriate motor and behavioral responses. The sensory processing of many children with ADHD is significantly affected, leading to either hypersensitivity (over-responsiveness) or hyposensitivity (under-responsiveness) to sensory stimuli. These unique sensory needs make creating sensory-friendly areas at home important, helping your child self-regulate and feel more at ease.

Neurodivergent children often experience sensory triggers that can lead to overstimulation or sensory overload. Common sensory sensitivities include loud noises, bright lights, strong smells, and certain textures. For example, a sudden loud noise may cause your child to cover their ears and become distressed, while certain fabrics can feel unbearably uncomfortable against their skin. Identifying these sensory triggers is the first step in creating a supportive environment. Observing your child's reactions and noting what causes discomfort can help you design spaces that minimize these triggers and promote a sense of calm.

Designing a sensory-friendly space involves careful consideration of your child's specific needs. Sensory tools, such as sensory toys and weighted blankets, can provide comfort and help your child manage sensory input. Fidget toys, like slime, stress balls, or spinners, can help your child focus by delivering a controlled outlet for their energy. Weighted blankets offer deep pressure stimulation, which can be calming and soothing, especially during moments of anxiety. Incorporating these tools into your child's daily routine can significantly affect their self-regulating ability.

Calming elements are another essential aspect of a sensory-friendly space. Soft lighting, such as dimmable or string lights, can create a soothing atmosphere. Harsh, bright lights can be overwhelming, so opt for lighting that can be adjusted to fit your child's needs. Gentle music or nature sounds can also provide a calming background, helping your child relax and focus. Consider using a white noise machine or a playlist of calming sounds to create a peaceful auditory environment. Soft textures, like plush rugs or cozy blankets, can further enhance the comfort of the space.

It is vital to create a safe space where your child can retreat when they feel overwhelmed. This area should be comfortable and inviting, with seating options that provide support and comfort. A bean bag chair or a large floor cushion can be perfect. Surround this space with soft textures and calming elements, making it a haven where your child can escape from sensory overload. This safe space can serve as a designated area for your child to relax, read a book, or take a break from the sensory demands of the day.

Incorporating sensory breaks into your child's routine can help them manage sensory overload and maintain focus throughout the day. Scheduled sensory breaks at regular intervals can provide opportunities for your child to engage in sensory activities that help them self-regulate. These breaks can include deep-pressure activities, such as using a weighted blanket or engaging in a bear hug, which can provide calming sensory input. Movement breaks, like jumping on a trampoline, playing with the family pet, or doing simple exercises, can also help your child release excess energy and reset their focus. Integrating these breaks into your daily schedule can create a more predictable and manageable routine for your child.

Adaptability and flexibility are essential when creating sensory-friendly spaces. Your child's sensory needs may change over time, so it's necessary to regularly assess and adjust the environment to ensure it continues to meet their needs. Regular assessments can involve checking whether the sensory space still provides the desired calming effect or if new tools or elements are needed. Parental observation is important in this process. Noting changes in your child's behavior and sensory responses can guide you in making necessary adjustments. This ongoing process of observation and adaptation ensures that the sensory-friendly space remains effective and supportive.

Creating sensory-friendly areas in your home can transform how your child experiences their environment. By understanding sensory processing, identifying sensory triggers, and designing spaces tailored to your child's needs, you can provide them with the tools and environment they need to thrive. Sensory tools, calming elements, and safe spaces can make a significant difference in helping your child manage sensory input and self-regulate. Incorporating sensory breaks and regularly adapting the environment ensures that these spaces continue to support your child's evolving needs.

As you continue to create a supportive home environment, remember that these efforts are not just about managing ADHD symptoms but also about fostering a sense of security and comfort for your child. The next chapter will explore emotional regulation and self-control, offering strategies to help your child navigate their emotions and develop coping skills that will serve them well throughout their lives.

EMOTIONAL REGULATION AND SELF-CONTROL

Imagine a world where your child can navigate their emotions with the grace of a seasoned traveler, recognizing what they feel and knowing precisely what to do about it. For many children with ADHD, emotions can feel like a stormy sea, unpredictable and overwhelming. Helping your child develop emotional regulation and self-control is not just about managing outbursts but teaching them to understand and navigate their inner world. This chapter provides practical tools and strategies to help your child develop these crucial skills, starting with the powerful practice of mindfulness.

STIMMING

Stimming, or self-stimulatory behavior, is a term often associated with individuals on the autism spectrum, but it also plays a significant role in ADHD. While stimming is sometimes misunderstood or seen as problematic, it can be a natural and important way for children with ADHD to manage their emotions, focus, and navigate their environment. Understanding stimming, its forms, and its role in helping these children thrive is crucial for parents, educators, and therapists alike.

Understanding Stimming

Stimming refers to repetitive movements, sounds, or behaviors that help regulate sensory input, manage emotions, or provide comfort. In children with ADHD, common stimming behaviors can include fidgeting, tapping, leg shaking, humming, or even repetitive speech patterns. These behaviors serve as outlets for the excess energy and heightened sensory input that many children with ADHD experience.

For neurotypical individuals, small acts like doodling, tapping a pencil, or twirling hair might go unnoticed. In contrast, for a child with ADHD, these behaviors are more pronounced, frequent, and necessary for self-regulation. Stimming helps children maintain focus and attention, offering an outlet for pent-up energy that might otherwise result in more disruptive behaviors.

Why Do Children with ADHD Stim?

ADHD is characterized by inattention, hyperactivity, and impulsivity. Stimming can be a response to these symptoms in several ways.

Energy Regulation: Children with ADHD often have high levels of physical energy that they struggle to channel appropriately. Stimming behaviors like bouncing a leg, tapping, or shifting in a seat can help release this energy in a controlled manner. It allows the child to stay seated or engaged in a task when they might otherwise feel the urge to move or get distracted.

Focus and Attention: For many children with ADHD, staying still can be counterproductive to focusing. Movement, even in small doses, helps keep their brains engaged. For instance, a child might doodle while listening to a lesson, allowing their hands to stay busy while their brain processes information. Without these small, repetitive movements, the brain can become restless, leading to daydreaming or distraction.

Emotional Regulation: Stimming can also serve as an emotional outlet. Children with ADHD often experience intense emotions and easily become overwhelmed or frustrated. Repetitive behaviors like humming, tapping, or rocking can be calming and soothing, offering a sense of control when emotions feel overwhelming.

Sensory Processing: ADHD can also come with sensory processing challenges. Some children may seek out additional sensory input (like pressure, sound, or movement) or may be sensitive to sensory overload. Stimming helps manage sensory needs by either providing the desired input or offering a predictable, soothing action in an environment that feels overwhelming.

The Importance of Accepting Stimming

Recognizing the positive role that stimming plays is essential. Unfortunately, some adults may see stimming behaviors as disruptive, distracting, or socially inappropriate and may try to stop or discourage them. However, suppressing stimming can be harmful, as it removes an essential tool for self-regulation and coping.

Rather than trying to eliminate stimming, it is important to understand when and why a child engages in these behaviors. Stimming can be a signal that the child is struggling with focus, feeling overwhelmed, or needing sensory input. By paying attention to these signals, adults can better understand the child's needs and provide support that aligns with those needs.

Types of Stimming in Children with ADHD

Stimming behaviors can vary widely from child to child, depending on their specific needs and preferences. Common types of stimming include:

Tactile Stimming: This includes behaviors like fidgeting with objects, rubbing hands together, twirling hair, or tapping fingers. For children with ADHD, tactile stimming often helps manage the need for physical movement and touch.

Auditory Stimming: Children might engage in humming, making repetitive noises, or tapping on surfaces. These sounds can help the child stay grounded or focused in situations where they need to concentrate.

Visual Stimming: Some children find visual stimulation calming or engaging. This can include activities like watching spinning objects, repeatedly drawing shapes or lines, or even blinking rhythmically.

Vestibular Stimming: This involves movements like rocking, swinging, or bouncing. These rhythmic movements help the child regulate their internal sense of balance and comfort.

Supporting Healthy Stimming in Children with ADHD

Supporting stimming involves striking a balance between allowing these behaviors and ensuring they do not interfere with daily life or learning. Here are some strategies to encourage healthy stimming:

Provide Structured Outlets for Movement: Incorporate breaks and physical activity into the child's routine. Scheduled movement breaks, access to sensory tools (like fidget spinners, stress balls, or putty), and opportunities to engage in active play can help satisfy the child's need for movement.

Create Stimming-Friendly Environments: At school or home, ensure that the child has spaces where stimming is not only accepted but encouraged. For example, allowing a child to quietly tap a pencil during class or offering a designated spot where they can engage in rocking or jumping without disruption.

Teach Self-Awareness and Regulation: As children grow older, they can be taught to recognize when and where certain stimming behaviors are more appropriate. For example, teaching a child to use quieter stims in public settings or encouraging them to take movement breaks when they feel restless helps them develop self-regulation skills.

Normalize Stimming: Reducing stigma around stimming is important. Help the child understand that everyone has coping mechanisms and that stimming is a normal and healthy way to manage their needs. Educating peers and teachers about the role of stimming can foster a more inclusive and supportive environment.

Monitor for Excessive Stimming: While stimming is generally healthy, excessive or harmful stimming (e.g., to the point of self-injury) may indicate deeper emotional distress or sensory overwhelm. In these cases, working with a therapist or occupational therapist to develop alternative strategies can be beneficial.

Stimming is a vital tool for children with ADHD, helping them navigate the world with greater ease. Instead of viewing these behaviors as problems to be fixed, it is essential to see them as adaptive strategies that support focus, emotional regulation, and sensory balance. By understanding and supporting healthy stimming, parents, educators, and therapists can better meet these children's needs, empowering them to thrive in various environments.

MINDFULNESS PRACTICES FOR ADHD KIDS

Mindfulness is a term you've likely heard, but what does it truly mean, especially for neurodivergent children? At its core, mindfulness is the practice of present-moment awareness. It involves paying full attention to what is happening immediately, without judgment. For children with ADHD, mindfulness can be transformative. It helps them enhance their focus, reduce stress, and improve emotional regulation. The benefits are multifaceted—improved focus allows them to stay present in tasks; reduced stress helps manage the anxiety that often accompanies ADHD; and emotional balance equips them to handle the highs and lows of their daily experiences.

Introducing mindfulness to children may seem challenging, but you can do it through simple, age-appropriate exercises. One effective practice is the body scan. This exercise involves guiding your child to notice sensations from head to toe. Have them close their eyes and take a few deep breaths. Then, starting from the top of their head, encourage them to focus on each part of their body, noticing any sensations—warmth, tingling, tension, or relaxation. This practice helps them connect with their bodily sensations and brings them into the present moment.

Mindful breathing is another excellent exercise. It focuses on the breath as an anchor to the present. Teach your child to take slow, deep breaths, paying attention to the air entering and leaving their lungs. This simple act of focusing on the breath can help calm their mind and reduce anxiety. Ask them to place a hand on their belly and feel it rise and fall with each breath, adding a tactile element to the exercise.

Exploring mindful feelings is a practice that encourages children to notice and name their emotions. Ask your child to sit quietly and reflect on how they are feeling at that moment. Guide them to recognize whether the feeling is positive or negative without judgment. This practice helps them become more aware of their emotional state and teaches them that all feelings are valid. By acknowledging their emotions, they can begin to understand and manage them better.

Mindful listening is an engaging way to practice mindfulness. Take your child outside or sit by an open window. Ask them to close their eyes and listen to the sounds around them. Whether it's birds chirping, the rustling of leaves, or distant traffic, encourage them to focus on each sound. This exercise sharpens their auditory awareness and helps them stay grounded in the present.

Incorporating mindfulness into daily routines can make these practices second nature. Start with mindful eating. Encourage your child to savor each meal bite, paying attention to the taste, texture, and aroma. This means no screens, music, or distractions—just the meal and the people at the table. This practice enhances their focus and promotes a healthy relationship with food.

Bedtime mindfulness can be a calming end to the day. Introduce calming exercises before sleep, such as a short body scan or mindful breathing. Use this time for executive function exercises, like reviewing the day and preparing for tomorrow. Ask your child simple questions like, "Are we ready for tomorrow?" These cues help them reflect and plan, reducing anxiety about the unknown.

Mindful walking is another practice to incorporate. Whether it's a short walk to the park or around the block, encourage your child to pay attention to each step. Have them notice the sensation of their feet touching the ground, the rhythm of their walk, and the environment around them. This practice turns a simple walk into a grounding and mindful experience.

Several mindfulness apps and resources are available to support you and your child in this practice. Apps like Headspace for Kids and Smiling Mind offer guided mindfulness exercises tailored for children. When integrated into your daily routine, these apps provide structured sessions. Online resources, such as guided mindfulness videos and printable exercises, can also be valuable tools. These resources offer a variety of practices, ensuring that you can find something that resonates with your child.

A quick and effective practice is a five-minute mindfulness meditation. Set aside just five minutes each day for this practice. Have your child sit comfortably, close their eyes, and focus on their breath. Guide them to notice the inhale and exhale, gently bringing their attention back to the breath whenever their mind wanders. This short practice can significantly improve their ability to focus and self-regulate.

Mindfulness is a powerful tool for helping children with ADHD navigate their emotions and improve their overall well-being. By introducing simple, age-appropriate mindfulness exercises and incorporating them into daily routines, you can help your child develop the skills they need to stay present, manage stress, and find emotional balance. The journey to emotional regulation and self-control is ongoing, but with mindfulness, you provide your child with a toolkit they can use throughout their lives.

BREATHING TECHNIQUES TO CALM EMOTIONAL STORMS

Breathing is more than just a primary bodily function; it's a powerful tool for emotional regulation, especially for children with ADHD. Even extreme-stress occupations like the Navy Seals and other Special Forces are trained in breathing techniques to calm their minds and make sound decisions. Controlled breathing can influence the nervous system, helping to calm the fight-or-flight response that often accompanies stress and anxiety. When your child faces a stressful situation, their body's natural reaction is to activate the sympathetic nervous system, which can lead to feelings of panic and loss of control. Controlled breathing techniques can activate the parasympathetic nervous system, which counteracts this response and promotes a state of calm. This immediate emotional relief is quick and effective, making breathing exercises an excellent strategy for managing emotional storms.

Teaching your child basic breathing techniques can empower them to take control of their emotions. One effective method is deep belly breathing. Encourage your child to take full breaths into their abdomen rather than shallow breaths into their chest. Have them place one hand on their stomach and the other on their chest. As they inhale deeply through their nose, their stomach should rise, and as they exhale through their mouth, their stomach should fall. This technique promotes relaxation and helps to ground them in the present moment.

Another valuable technique is 4-7-8 breathing. Guide your child to inhale for a count of four, hold their breath for a count of seven, and then exhale slowly for a count of eight. This method can be handy for reducing anxiety and promoting a sense of calm. It might feel a bit challenging at first, but with practice, your child can master this technique and use it whenever they need to calm themselves.

Box breathing is another simple yet effective technique. Instruct your child to inhale for a count of four, hold their breath for a count of four, exhale for a count of four, and then hold their breath again for a count of four. This rhythmic pattern can help regulate their breathing and provide a sense of structure and control, which can be incredibly soothing during moments of distress.

These breathing techniques help your child manage their emotions when applied in various situations. Before a test, for instance, practicing deep belly breathing can reduce anxiety and improve focus. Encourage your child to take a few minutes to breathe deeply before entering the classroom. During a tantrum, 4-7-8 breathing can help your child regain control. Guide them through the counts, providing a calm and steady presence. In social situations, box breathing can help manage nervousness. If your child feels overwhelmed at a birthday party or family gathering, remind them to use their box breathing to stay calm and collected.

Creating a breathing toolkit can further support your child in using these techniques independently. Assemble a set of breathing cards with step-by-step instructions for each method. These cards can be kept in a pocket or backpack, making them easily accessible whenever your child needs them. Visual reminders, such as posters or stickers placed around the house, can be gentle prompts to practice breathing exercises regularly. The toolkit can also include portable tools like stress balls or calming scents. These items can provide additional sensory input that complements the breathing techniques, enhancing their calming effect.

Breathing Toolkit Ideas

1. **Breathing Cards**: Step-by-step instructions for each technique, laminated for durability.
2. **Visual Reminders**: Posters or stickers with simple prompts like "Breathe" or images of the breathing patterns.
3. **Portable Tools**: Stress balls, essential oil rollers, small sensory toys, and breathing exercises.

These tools can be a constant companion for your child, offering comfort and guidance when they need it most. Equipping your child with these resources empowers them to navigate their emotions and build resilience.

Incorporating these breathing techniques into your child's daily routine can make them a natural part of their emotional regulation toolkit. Encourage your child to practice these exercises regularly, even when not feeling stressed, so they become second nature. The more familiar and comfortable they are with these techniques, the more effective they will be in moments of need. This proactive approach can help your child develop a sense of mastery over their emotions, fostering confidence and self-control.

TOOLS FOR IDENTIFYING AND EXPRESSING FEELINGS

Helping children recognize their emotions is fundamental in fostering emotional regulation. Emotional awareness enables them to understand their feelings and why, which is crucial for managing their reactions. Start by teaching your child to identify different feelings. You can use everyday moments as opportunities for this. When your child seems upset, ask them to describe their feelings. Are they angry, sad, or frustrated? This practice helps them connect physical sensations and behaviors with specific emotions.

Emotion charts are excellent visual aids for identifying emotions. These charts typically feature faces with different expressions labeled with the corresponding emotion. Place an emotion chart in a common area, like the fridge or their bedroom wall. Encourage your child to point to the face that matches how they feel. Labeling their emotions can help children become more aware of their feelings and better understand their emotional landscape. Additionally, using humor can often defuse big negative emotions. A well-timed joke or a funny face can lighten the mood and make it easier for your child to open up about what's bothering them.

Journaling is another effective tool for emotional identification. Encourage your child to write about their daily feelings. It doesn't have to be a detailed diary entry; even a few sentences or drawings about their day can be illuminating. Journaling provides a safe space for self-expression and can help children process their emotions. It also allows you to gain insights into their emotional world, making it easier to offer appropriate support.

Once your child can recognize their emotions, the next step is to provide appropriate tools for expressing them. An emotion wheel, a visual tool that helps children explore the range of their feelings, can be handy. Emotion wheels typically feature a central circle with basic emotions, branching into more complex feelings. This tool helps children move beyond basic emotions like "happy" or "sad" and explore more nuanced feelings. For example, they might start with "angry" and move outwards to "frustrated" or "irritated."

Associating common feelings with topics they enjoy can make emotional expression more relatable. If your child loves dinosaurs, you can create a chart where different dinosaurs represent different emotions. For instance, a T-Rex could symbolize anger, while a Triceratops represents calm. This playful approach makes discussing emotions less intimidating and more engaging for your child. Drawing or painting can also serve as creative outlets for expressing feelings. Provide your child with art supplies and encourage them to express their emotions through artwork. This non-verbal form of expression can be particularly beneficial for children who struggle to articulate their feelings with words.

Role-playing is another powerful tool. Create safe scenarios where your child can practice expressing their emotions. For example, you can role-play a situation in which they feel angry or sad and guide them through appropriate ways to express those feelings. This practice builds emotional vocabulary and equips them with strategies to handle real-life situations.

Developing a robust feelings vocabulary is essential for precise and effective communication. Encourage your child to expand their emotional vocabulary beyond basic terms. Introduce more specific emotion words like "disappointed," "excited," or "anxious." Children can understand and use advanced vocabulary, and providing these words can empower them to communicate their feelings more accurately. Descriptive language is vital for children with ADHD, as it leaves little room for ambiguity. Exact terminology helps them understand and convey their emotions concisely.

To reinforce this vocabulary, engage in communication exercises that use emotion words in sentences. For example, you can create flashcards with different emotion words and practice forming sentences together. This exercise improves their vocabulary and enhances their ability to communicate effectively. When your child can articulate their feelings precisely, it alleviates frustration for both them and you as a parent.

Creating a supportive environment for emotional expression is crucial. Active listening plays a significant role in this. When your child wants to talk, give them your full attention. Put down your phone, pause the TV show, and focus entirely on what they say. This act shows them that their feelings matter and that you are there to support them. Validating their feelings is equally important. Acknowledge and accept their emotions without judgment. Say, "I see you're upset right now, and that's okay." Reinforcing positive emotions and interactions while explaining that negative emotions can become unproductive if we don't manage them well which may lead to conflict. This explanation can help them understand the impact of their reactions.

Open communication should be a regular part of your family's routine. Encourage emotional check-ins in a disarming or casual environment, such as during a walk or while doing a shared activity. Avoid doing this right after school or in other high-stress situations, as children tend to give answers that move the conversation along rather than diving into their true feelings.

Creating a safe and supportive environment where your child feels comfortable expressing their emotions is critical to helping them develop emotional regulation and self-control.

By teaching your child to recognize and express their emotions, providing a robust feelings vocabulary, and fostering a supportive environment, you equip them with the tools they need for emotional regulation. These skills are not just beneficial for managing ADHD but are essential for their overall well-being and development. Next, we will explore strategies for positive reinforcement and behavior management, continuing our journey towards creating a supportive and nurturing environment for your ADHD super-kid.

POSITIVE REINFORCEMENT AND BEHAVIOR MANAGEMENT

Imagine you're in a garden, nurturing a delicate flower that requires just the right amount of sunlight, water, and care to blossom. Parenting a child is much like tending to that flower. It demands patience, understanding, and a keen eye for what helps your child thrive. Positive reinforcement and behavior management play vital roles in this nurturing process. These strategies can shape your child's behavior, encouraging positive actions while gently steering them away from less desirable ones.

AVOID MEDICATION UNTIL ALL OTHER OPTIONS ARE EXHAUSTED

While medication can be a quick fix, it's vital to explore all other avenues before turning to pharmaceutical solutions. Supplements like omega-3 fatty acids, magnesium, iron, and zinc have shown promise in reducing ADHD symptoms. for brain health and can improve focus and cognitive function. Magnesium helps regulate neurotransmitters, which send signals throughout the nervous system, while iron is crucial for dopamine production, a neurotransmitter involved in attention and reward processes. Zinc plays a role in modulating brain activity and neurotransmission. Incorporating these supplements into your child's diet can provide a natural alternative to medication, offering benefits without the side effects of pharmaceutical options. Check with your pediatricians to ensure a healthy dosage for your child's age, weight, and other health factors.

ADHD stimulants, while effective for some, come with a range of potential side effects that can impact your child's well-being. Common side effects include reduced appetite, leading to nutritional deficiencies and weight loss. Overstimulation is another concern—the medication can make your child feel jittery or anxious, exacerbating issues rather than alleviating them. Dehydration is also a risk, as stimulants can suppress thirst signals, leading to inadequate fluid intake. These side effects can create additional challenges, making it essential to weigh the benefits against the potential drawbacks.

Moreover, the prevalence of substance abuse disorders among kids prescribed ADHD stimulants raises serious concerns. According to a study by the National Institute on Drug Abuse (NIDA), children with ADHD who are prescribed stimulants are at a higher risk for developing substance use disorders later in life. This risk presents a challenge, particularly when considering the long-term implications of medication. The study emphasizes combining medication with behavioral therapies to mitigate this risk. It's a stark reminder that while medication can be part of the solution, it should not be the sole approach.

These considerations make exploring natural supplements and behavioral strategies even more crucial. Before resorting to medication, it's worth trying other methods that can provide relief without the associated risks. For instance, integrating a balanced diet rich in these essential nutrients can support brain health and improve ADHD symptoms. Encouraging physical activity is another natural approach that can significantly benefit children with ADHD. Exercise helps regulate mood, improve focus, and reduce hyperactivity, providing a holistic way to manage symptoms.

In addition to dietary and lifestyle changes, behavioral interventions play a critical role. Positive reinforcement, clear expectations, and consistent routines can create a supportive environment that fosters positive behavior. These methods help children develop self-regulation skills, making it easier for them to manage their symptoms without relying solely on medication.

Interactive Element: Supplement Tracker

Creating a supplement tracker can help you monitor the impact of natural supplements on your child's behavior and symptoms. Here's a simple template to get you started.

1. **Supplement**: Omega-3

   - **Frequency**: Once daily
   - **Notes**: Monitor for improvements in focus and cognitive function

2. **Supplement**: Magnesium

   - **Frequency**: Once daily
   - **Notes**: Observe any changes in mood and relaxation

3. **Supplement**: Iron

   - **Frequency**: Once daily
   - **Notes**: Watch for increased energy levels and attention span

4. **Supplement**: Zinc

   - **Frequency**: Once daily
   - **Notes**: Check for improvements in overall brain activity and neurotransmission

This tracker can help you keep a record of what works best for your child, making it easier to tailor their supplementation for optimal results. Check with your pediatrician to ensure a proper dosage is being utilized.

Considering all options before resorting to medication can empower you to make informed decisions that best support your child's health and well-being. By exploring natural supplements, monitoring the potential side effects of medication, and understanding the risks associated with long-term use, you can create a balanced approach to managing ADHD. This holistic perspective ensures that you're not just treating symptoms but nurturing your child's overall development and well-being.

CREATING EFFECTIVE BEHAVIOR CHARTS

Behavior charts can be a game-changer for managing ADHD symptoms. They provide a visual and tangible way for children to see their progress and understand the rewards of positive behavior. When you create a behavior chart, think of it as a roadmap guiding your child toward better habits and self-regulation. The key to an effective behavior chart is clarity and consistency. Start by identifying the specific behaviors you want to encourage or discourage. These should be clear, measurable, and achievable. For example, instead of a vague goal like "be good," opt for "complete homework before dinner" or "use inside voice during meals."

Once you've pinpointed the behaviors, the next step is to design the chart. These charts can be as straightforward or as creative as you like. Some parents use a basic grid with days of the week and specific tasks, while others incorporate colorful stickers and illustrations to make it more engaging. The important thing is that the chart is easy for your child to understand and use. Place it in a visible spot where your child can easily see it, like on the refrigerator or in their bedroom. This constant visibility reinforces your targeted behaviors and keeps your child engaged.

Tracking progress is crucial. Each time your child exhibits the desired behavior, mark it on the chart. The tracker could be with a sticker, a checkmark, or a smiley face—whatever resonates most with your child. The act of marking the chart should be a moment of celebration. Praise your child and acknowledge their effort. This immediate positive feedback is essential for reinforcing the behavior. Over time, your child will associate the behavior with positive outcomes, making them more likely to repeat it.

Consistency is key. Regularly update the chart and review it daily with your child. Consistency keeps them engaged and provides opportunities for reflection and discussion. If a particular behavior isn't marked off as often as you'd like, use this to discuss any challenges your child may face. Perhaps the goal needs to be adjusted to be more attainable, or external factors may impact your child's ability to meet it. Open communication ensures the chart remains a helpful tool rather than a source of frustration.

Incorporating rewards into the behavior chart can further motivate your child. These rewards don't have to be extravagant. Small, meaningful incentives can be incredibly effective. You might offer extra screen time, a special outing, or a small toy as a reward for consistently meeting behavior goals. Tailoring these rewards to your child's interests and preferences is essential to keep them motivated. Additionally, varying the rewards can keep things exciting and prevent your child from losing interest over time.

Interactive Element: Behavior Chart Template

Creating your behavior chart can be fun, and you can include your child. Here's a basic template to get you started.

1. **Behavior Goal**: Complete homework before dinner

   - **Days of the Week**: Monday, Tuesday, Wednesday, Thursday, and Friday
   - **Tracking Method**: Stickers or checkmarks

2. **Behavior Goal**: Use inside voice during meals

   - **Days of the Week**: Monday, Tuesday, Wednesday, Thursday, and Friday
   - **Tracking Method**: Smileys or stars

3. **Reward**: Thirty minutes of extra screen time on Saturday for meeting weekly goals

Customize this template to fit your child's needs and preferences. Involving your child in creating the chart can also increase their sense of ownership and commitment to the process. My kids loved helping me create ours, and their creativity shone through.

Troubleshooting common issues with behavior charts is part of the process. If you notice your child's interest waning or the desired behaviors not improving, consider varying the rewards to keep the system engaging. Introducing new rewards every couple of months can keep things fresh. Adjusting goals to ensure they are achievable and relevant is also crucial. Start small and scale upwards; it's easier to build on success than to constantly reset expectations. Maintaining consistency across all caregivers is vital. If one caregiver is less diligent about updating the chart or enforcing the rewards, it can undermine the system. Ensuring everyone involved is on board and committed to the process will provide the stability and reinforcement your child needs.

USING POSITIVE REINFORCEMENT TO BUILD GOOD HABITS

Positive reinforcement is a powerful tool in shaping behavior, particularly for children with ADHD. The concept is straightforward yet profoundly effective—encourage desired behaviors by rewarding them, increasing the likelihood that your child will repeat them. For children with ADHD, who often struggle with impulsivity and attention, positive reinforcement provides clear, immediate feedback that can guide them toward better habits. The psychological principles behind positive reinforcement are rooted in behaviorism, which posits that behaviors followed by positive outcomes are more likely to be repeated. This method leverages reward-based motivation, making it particularly effective for ADHD kids who thrive on immediate gratification.

Immediate rewards play a crucial role in positive reinforcement. Children with ADHD often have difficulty delaying gratification, so providing instant rewards can be highly motivating. For instance, if your child completes their homework without reminders, offering a small reward like a sticker or small candy/treat immediately reinforces the desired behavior. Over time, these immediate rewards can help build intrinsic motivation, encouraging your child to engage in positive behaviors even without external incentives. The goal is to gradually reduce the reliance on rewards as your child begins to internalize the value of the behavior itself.

Identifying appropriate rewards is essential to the success of positive reinforcement. Different children are motivated by different things, so choosing meaningful and motivating rewards for your child is necessary. Tangible rewards like stickers, small toys, or something related to their favorite hobby can be very effective. For example, if your child is into collecting action figures, earning a new figure for consistent good behavior can be highly motivating. Sweets can also work, though it's wise to use them sparingly to avoid health issues.

Social rewards can be equally powerful. Simple acts of praise, high-fives, or even Facetime or Skype calls to grandparents, aunts, and uncles to share an achievement can make a big difference. These social rewards reinforce the behavior and strengthen your child's social bonds, providing a sense of belonging and support. Activity-based rewards are another great option. Extra playtime, special outings, or the privilege of choosing the family meal can be highly motivating. These rewards offer the added benefit of creating positive family experiences, further reinforcing the desired behaviors.

Implementing a positive reinforcement system involves several steps. Start by setting clear goals. Define specific behaviors you want to encourage, such as "complete homework without reminders" or "use polite words during meals." These goals should be clear, measurable, and achievable. Once you have set the goals, track progress using a log. This log doesn't always have to be visible to your child; sometimes, keeping it private reduces pressure and makes the process feel more natural. Decide on a reward schedule, whether immediate or delayed, and stick to it. Immediate rewards are for more minor, daily achievements, while delayed rewards are for long-term goals.

Troubleshooting common issues is part of maintaining an effective system. One challenge parents often face is fading interest in rewards. To keep the system engaging, vary the rewards. Have a list of ten to fifteen potential rewards and introduce two or three new ones every couple of months. Replace any rewards that could be more motivating. Adjusting goals is also crucial. Ensure they are achievable and relevant. Start small; it's much easier to scale upwards than to constantly reset expectations. Consistency across all caregivers is vital. Kids quickly learn to vary their behavior based on who is watching, so ensure everyone involved is on the same page.

Maintaining consistency ensures that the reinforcement system remains effective. Inconsistencies can confuse your child and undermine the system's effectiveness. Ensure all caregivers are committed to the process and follow the same guidelines. Regular check-ins reinforce this consistency and address any issues that arise.

MANAGING IMPULSIVITY: STRATEGIES THAT WORK

Impulsivity is a hallmark of ADHD, making everyday life a bit more unpredictable for your child and your family. At its core, impulsivity is acting without thinking. It's the urge to do something immediately without considering the consequences. Children with ADHD often struggle with this, leading to behaviors like interrupting conversations or reacting negatively when asked to do a task. Imagine your child blurting out an answer in class without raising their hand or suddenly grabbing a toy from a sibling without asking. These impulsive actions can create social and academic challenges, affecting your child's relationships and performance in school.

Teaching impulse control is important. One effective strategy is the "stop and think" method. Encourage your child to pause before acting. You can practice this together in low-stress situations, like taking a moment before deciding which game to play. Another helpful technique is self-talk, which involves encouraging positive internal dialogue. Teach your child to remind themselves to stay calm or think things through silently. For example, before reacting to a frustrating situation, they might say internally, "I need to take a deep breath and think about what to do next."

Delay of gratification exercises can also be beneficial. These exercises involve practicing and waiting for rewards. Start with something simple, like waiting a few minutes before eating a favorite snack. Gradually increase the waiting time as your child becomes more comfortable with the concept. This practice can help them develop patience and better manage their impulses.

Creating a structured environment helps manage impulsivity. Establishing clear rules and expectations sets boundaries that your child can understand and follow. Consistent routines provide stability, making it easier for your child to anticipate what comes next and prepare mentally. For example, having a set bedtime routine helps them know it's time to wind down, reducing the likelihood of impulsive behaviors at night. Supervised activities ensure that your child is in a safe and controlled setting. This supervision can help redirect impulsive actions into more constructive behaviors.

Modeling self-control is one of the most powerful tools at your disposal. Children learn a great deal by observing the adults around them. Demonstrate calm and thoughtful behavior in your own actions. If you feel frustrated, show your child how you take a deep breath and think before responding. Praise and rewards for their efforts to control impulses can reinforce positive behavior. Acknowledging even small successes will encourage your child to keep trying. For example, if they wait their turn during a game, praise them and offer a small reward.

Role-playing scenarios can provide a safe space for your child to practice impulse control. Create situations where your children may act impulsively and guide them through appropriate responses. For instance, you can role-play a scenario where they want to interrupt a conversation. Practice waiting and politely saying, "Excuse me" instead. These rehearsals help build their confidence and prepare them for real-life situations.

Managing impulsivity involves a multi-faceted approach. By understanding what impulsivity is and why it occurs, teaching impulse control techniques, creating a structured environment, and modeling self-control, you can help your child navigate this challenging aspect of ADHD. Consistent praise and role-playing further reinforce these lessons, providing your child with the tools they need to succeed.

Incorporating these strategies for managing impulsivity can make a tangible difference in your child's daily life. By fostering impulse control and creating a supportive environment, you set the stage for positive behavior patterns. As we progress, we'll explore the importance of improving social skills and building relationships, continuing our path toward a stable and nurturing environment for your ADHD super-kid.

IMPROVING SOCIAL SKILLS AND RELATIONSHIPS

Imagine your child standing on the edge of a playground, eyes wide with curiosity yet hesitant to step forward. They watch other kids laughing and playing, but something holds them back. For many neurodivergent children, social interactions can be a daunting terrain to navigate. Unlike academic challenges, social skills don't come with clear instructions, making them harder to master. Yet, understanding social cues and body language is crucial for effective communication and relationship-building. This chapter will equip you with the tools and strategies to help your child decode the often-unspoken language of social interactions.

TEACHING SOCIAL CUES AND BODY LANGUAGE

Understanding social cues is essential for anyone looking to build strong relationships. For children with ADHD, this can be particularly challenging. Social cues include facial expressions, tone of voice, and body posture. These non-verbal signals significantly influence how we communicate and understand each other.

Children with ADHD may struggle to recognize these cues, making it difficult for them to respond appropriately in social situations. This lack of perception can lead to misunderstandings, social isolation, and frustration for the child and those around them.

Recognizing facial expressions is a foundational skill in interpreting emotions. When someone smiles, frowns, or raises an eyebrow, they communicate a wealth of information without saying a word. For neurodivergent children, these cues can be subtle and easily missed. Teaching your child to identify emotions through facial expressions can start with simple exercises. Use emotion flashcards that depict different facial expressions. Show these cards to your child and ask them to identify the emotion being expressed. Over time, this practice can help them become more attuned to the emotional states of others.

Understanding tone of voice is another crucial aspect of interpreting social cues. How something is said can carry as much meaning as the words themselves. A sarcastic remark, a gentle reassurance, or an angry outburst are all conveyed through tone. Children with ADHD may take words at face value, missing the underlying emotion. To help your child interpret vocal cues, engage in activities where you read sentences in different tones of voice. Ask your child to guess the emotion behind each tone. This exercise can sharpen their ability to discern feelings and intentions in conversations.

Interpreting body posture is equally important. Body language can reveal a person's level of interest, comfort, or engagement in a conversation. A slouched posture may indicate boredom, while leaning forward can show interest. Neurodivergent children often focus on the literal message and may overlook these physical signals. Observe people in different settings together to teach your child about body posture. Point out how someone's posture changes based on their mood or the situation. Discuss what these body language cues might mean. This observational practice can enhance your child's ability to read non-verbal signals.

To further aid in recognizing and interpreting emotions, incorporate specific exercises and activities into your child's routine. Mirror exercises can be beneficial as they give immediate feedback. Stand in front of a mirror with your child and make different facial expressions. Have your child mimic these expressions and label the emotions they represent. This hands-on approach helps them connect facial movements with emotional states. Emotion games can also be engaging. Read stories or watch movies together and pause to discuss the characters' feelings. Ask your child to identify the emotions based on facial expressions, tone of voice, and body posture. These activities make learning about emotions fun and interactive.

Teaching appropriate body language involves understanding and respecting personal space, using and recognizing gestures, and maintaining eye contact. Personal space is a concept that can be tricky for children with ADHD. They might stand too close or far from others, making interactions uncomfortable. Explain the idea of personal space using visual aids like hula hoops to illustrate the distance that feels comfortable in different situations. Practice standing at appropriate distances in various scenarios, such as talking to a friend or greeting a teacher.

Gestures are another critical component of body language. They can emphasize a point, show agreement, or convey confusion. Children with ADHD may not use gestures effectively or may misinterpret those of others. Role-playing exercises help practice nonverbal communicative gestures outside the usual head shake or nod—a shrug, the "OK" hand gesture, or thumbs-up.

Encourage your child to incorporate these gestures into daily interactions, enhancing communication skills.

Eye contact is a powerful form of non-verbal communication. It shows interest, confidence, and engagement. However, maintaining eye contact can be challenging for children with ADHD. They may find it uncomfortable or forget to make eye contact altogether. Practice eye contact through simple games. For example, have a staring contest to see who can maintain eye contact the longest. Gradually increase the duration and encourage your child to use eye contact in conversations. Praise their efforts to reinforce this crucial social skill.

Social stories and visual aids can further support your child's understanding of social cues and appropriate responses. Social stories are custom narratives based on real-life situations your child might encounter. These stories describe the setting, the people involved, and the expected behaviors. For instance, a social story about attending a birthday party can outline how to greet the host, participate in games, and thank the host before leaving. Reading and discussing these stories can prepare your child for similar real-life situations. It's like studying for a test; familiarity with a topic or scenario equips our children with a valuable tool to navigate everyday interactions no matter how mundane or high stress.

Visual aids like charts and posters depicting social interactions can also be beneficial. Create a chart that shows different social scenarios and the appropriate responses. For example, a chart could illustrate how to join a conversation, share toys, or ask for help. Place these visual aids in common areas where your child can easily see them. They serve as constant reminders of the social cues and behaviors our children are learning.

Role-play cards are another valuable tool. These cards present various social scenarios and prompt your child to practice appropriate responses. For example, a card may describe a situation where a friend is upset, and your child needs to show empathy. Role-playing these scenarios helps your child rehearse social interactions in a safe and controlled environment. It builds their confidence and prepares them for real-life situations.

Interactive Element: Emotion Flashcards

Emotion flashcards can be a fun and educational tool for teaching your child to recognize and interpret facial expressions. Create a set of flashcards with different facial expressions and the corresponding emotions. Use these cards in various activities, such as matching games or storytelling sessions. This interactive approach helps reinforce emotional awareness and makes learning engaging.

Understanding social cues and body language is essential for effective communication and relationship-building. By teaching your child to recognize facial expressions, interpret vocal cues, and read body posture, you equip them with the tools they need to navigate social interactions. Incorporating exercises, visual aids, and role-playing scenarios can make this learning process enjoyable and effective. Your support and guidance in developing these skills can make a significant difference in your child's social life, helping them build meaningful relationships and thrive in social settings.

ROLE-PLAYING SCENARIOS TO PRACTICE SOCIAL SKILLS

Role-playing offers a safe and controlled environment for children with ADHD to practice social skills. It allows them to rehearse positive interactions, reducing anxiety when similar situations arise in real life. Imagine your child stepping into a social scenario with the confidence of an actor who has rehearsed their lines. This practice builds confidence and provides immediate feedback, helping your child learn and adjust their behavior in real time. Role-playing serves as a rehearsal that prepares them for the unpredictability of social interactions, making these encounters less daunting.

Creating realistic role-play scenarios tailored to the social challenges your child faces can be incredibly effective. Start with everyday school interactions. For instance, practice how to join a group. Set the scene by describing a group of kids playing a game. Guide your child to approach the group, make eye contact, and ask to join. Another practical scenario is asking for help. Whether asking a teacher for assistance with a difficult assignment or seeking help from a peer, practicing this can make it less intimidating. Move on to playground situations, such as sharing and taking turns. Use toys or games to simulate these interactions, teaching your child the importance of patience and fairness. Family gatherings present another set of challenges. Practice greeting relatives, starting conversations, and showing interest in others' lives. These scenarios help your child navigate the social intricacies of family events, making them more enjoyable and less stressful.

Guiding and facilitating role-plays effectively requires a thoughtful approach. Begin by setting the scene. Describe the context in detail so your child can visualize the scenario. For example, if practicing a school interaction, explain the setting: "You're in the classroom, and it's time for group work." Provide prompts to help your child with dialogue. Suggest phrases they can use if they struggle to find the right words. Encourage them to use these prompts, gradually building their confidence to initiate conversations independently. Offering feedback is vital. Use positive reinforcement to acknowledge what they did well. Constructive criticism should be gentle and specific. Instead of saying, "That wasn't right," try, "Next time, try making eye contact when you ask to join the group." This approach helps them understand what to improve without feeling discouraged.

Role-playing can also address specific social issues your child may be facing. If your child struggles with handling teasing, create a scenario where they practice responding appropriately. Teach them to stay calm, use assertive language, and seek help if needed. Role-play making new friends by practicing approaching someone, introducing themselves, and starting a conversation. Use different scenarios to keep the practice engaging and relevant. Conflict resolution is another critical area—practice scenarios where they must resolve disagreements, whether over a game or a group project. Teach them to listen to the other person's perspective, express their feelings calmly, and find a compromise.

Interactive Element: Role-Play Cards

Create a set of role-play cards to make this practice more engaging. Each card should describe a different social scenario and prompt your child to act it out. For example:

1. **Scenario**: Joining a group at recess.

    - **Prompt**: "You see a group of kids playing tag. How do you ask to join them?"

2. **Scenario**: Asking a teacher for help.

   - **Prompt**: "You don't understand a math problem. What do you say to the teacher?"

3. **Scenario**: Handling teasing.

   - **Prompt**: "A classmate teases you about your new haircut. How do you respond?"

Use these cards regularly to practice various social skills, making the learning process dynamic and interactive.

Using role-playing to practice social skills provides children with a valuable opportunity to rehearse and refine their interactions. By creating realistic scenarios, guiding the practice, and addressing specific social challenges, you can help your child build the confidence and skills they need to navigate social situations successfully. Role-playing prepares them for real-life interactions and empowers them to approach social encounters with a newfound sense of assurance and competence.

BUILDING AND MAINTAINING FRIENDSHIPS

Friendships are the cornerstone of a child's emotional and social development, and for children with ADHD, they hold even more significance. Friends provide emotional support, a buffer against stress, and a sense of belonging. Having someone to confide in and share experiences with can make a world of difference. It helps children feel understood and valued. Social learning is another critical aspect of friendships. Through interactions with peers, children learn essential social skills such as cooperation, empathy, and conflict resolution. They observe and mimic behaviors, gaining insights into social norms and expectations. This learning process is particularly beneficial for children with ADHD, who may struggle with understanding these unspoken rules. Friends also play a pivotal role in building self-esteem. Positive peer reinforcement can boost a child's confidence and sense of self-worth. Compliments, shared laughter, and mutual support create a positive feedback loop, reinforcing good behaviors and providing a sense of achievement.

Helping children with ADHD initiate friendships can be challenging but immensely rewarding. Finding common interests is a great starting point. Encourage your child to join clubs or groups that align with their hobbies and passions, whether a sports team, an art class, or a coding club. These settings provide natural opportunities for interaction and collaboration. Conversation starters can also be a helpful tool. Practice simple opening lines with your child, such as "Hi, I'm [Name]. What's your favorite game?" or "I noticed you like [Activity]. Can you tell me more about it?" These icebreakers can make initiating conversations more manageable. Encouraging social activities like playdates or group outings can further facilitate friendships. Arrange informal gatherings where children can play and interact in a relaxed environment. These activities provide a backdrop for children to get to know each other and form connections.

Maintaining friendships requires ongoing effort and communication. Regular communication is critical. Teach your child the importance of staying in touch with friends through phone calls, video chats, or handwritten notes. These small gestures help strengthen the bond and show they value the friendship. Conflict resolution is another crucial skill. Disagreements are inevitable but handling them well can strengthen friendships. Teach your child to listen to their friend's perspective, express their feelings calmly, and work together to find a solution. Practice these skills through role-playing or discussing hypothetical scenarios. Showing appreciation is equally essential. Encourage your child to recognize and value their friends' qualities and actions. Simple acts of gratitude, like saying "Thank you" or giving a small gift, can go a long way in nurturing friendships.

As a parent, you play a vital role in supporting your child's social life. Hosting playdates is a practical way to create opportunities for socializing. Plan activities your child and their friends will enjoy, ensuring the environment is welcoming and inclusive. Encourage extracurricular activities such as sports, arts, or clubs. These activities provide structured settings for social interaction, helping your child build friendships around shared interests. Monitoring social media use is also crucial. Ensure that your child's online interactions are positive and age-appropriate. Teach them about online etiquette and the importance of respectful communication. Be aware of the potential for cyberbullying and take steps to protect your child from negative online experiences.

Friendships are vital for a child's emotional and social development, offering emotional support, social learning opportunities, and a boost to self-esteem. Helping your child initiate and maintain friendships involves finding common interests, practicing conversation starters, and encouraging social activities. Regular communication, conflict resolution, and showing appreciation are vital to nurturing these relationships. Your support as a parent, through hosting playdates, encouraging extracurricular activities, and monitoring social media use, can significantly impact your child's ability to build and maintain meaningful friendships.

In the next chapter, we will explore strategies for collaborating with educators and schools to ensure your child receives the support they need in an academic setting.

COLLABORATING WITH EDUCATORS AND SCHOOLS

Imagine your child navigating a maze, each turn filled with promise and challenge. This maze is their educational journey, and as their guide, you need the right tools to help them succeed. Collaborating with educators and schools is like finding a map that lights the way through this intricate path. When your child has ADHD, this collaboration becomes even more crucial. Schools are not just places of learning; they are environments where your child's strengths can shine, and their challenges can be managed effectively. Understanding and advocating for Individualized Education Programs (IEPs) and 504 Plans is essential to ensure your child receives the support they deserve.

ADVOCATING FOR IEPS AND 504 PLANS

Understanding the purpose and benefits of IEPs and 504 Plans is the first step in securing your child's support. An Individualized Education Program (IEP) is a customized educational plan tailored to meet the unique needs of students with disabilities, including ADHD. The goal of an IEP is to provide specialized instruction and services that enable the student to succeed in the general education curriculum. This plan is legally binding and must be reviewed and updated annually to ensure it continues to meet the student's evolving needs.

A 504 Plan, however, focuses on providing accommodations to ensure that students with disabilities have equal access to education. Unlike an IEP, which often includes specialized instruction, a 504 Plan typically provides for modifications to the learning environment or teaching methods. These accommodations help your child fully participate in the general education classroom and can include extended test times, preferential seating, and adjustments to homework assignments.

Obtaining an IEP or 504 Plan begins with a formal request to the school. This request should be in writing and addressed to your child's teacher, school counselor, or principal. Be specific about your concerns and why you believe your child needs an IEP or 504 Plan. Once the request is submitted, the school will initiate an evaluation process. This evaluation typically involves educational and psychological assessments conducted by school psychologists and other specialists. These assessments aim to understand your child's strengths and areas of need, providing a comprehensive picture of their educational challenges.

Documentation plays a crucial role in this process. Gather medical records, teacher observations, and previous assessments highlighting your child's struggles and successes. Teacher observations are particularly valuable as they provide insights into how your child functions in a classroom setting. This documentation supports the case for why your child needs specific accommodations or specialized instruction.

An effective IEP or 504 Plan should be comprehensive and tailored to your child's unique needs. Specific accommodations are a key component. For example, extended test times can help your child manage their time better and reduce anxiety during exams. Preferential seating can minimize distractions by placing your child closer to the teacher. Reducing noise and visual stimuli in the classroom can create a more focused learning environment, making it easier for your child to concentrate.

Goals and objectives are another critical element. These should be measurable academic and behavioral targets that provide clear benchmarks for your child's progress. For instance, an educational goal may be to improve reading comprehension skills by a certain percentage over the school year. Behavioral goals may include specific strategies for managing impulsivity or enhancing social interactions. Regularly reviewing these goals ensures that the plan remains relevant and effective.

Support services are also essential. These include speech therapy, occupational therapy, and regular guidance counselor assessments. For example, weekly or bimonthly sessions with a guidance counselor can reinforce emotional regulation and social skills strategies. Occupational therapy could focus on improving fine motor skills, which can benefit tasks like writing. Speech therapy can address communication challenges, helping your child express themselves more clearly and confidently.

Advocating for your child during IEP or 504 Plan meetings is critical. Preparing a list of concerns beforehand ensures that you address all key issues. Be specific about what you've observed at home and what teachers have reported. Bringing support, such as an advocate or specialist, can provide additional expertise and reinforce your points. Advocacy can include professionals who understand ADHD and can offer insights into effective strategies.

Keeping detailed records of all communications and decisions is essential. Document every meeting, email, and phone call related to your child's education plan. This record-keeping ensures a clear history of what has been discussed and agreed upon. It also provides a reference if any issues arise in the future.

Persistence is key, especially when dealing with public schools, which may sometimes minimize or downplay your concerns. Be firm and consistent in your advocacy. Emphasize the positive tactics that will ensure your child's success. If the proposed accommodation or service is not working, don't hesitate to request a review or adjustment. Your child's needs may change, and their educational plan should be flexible enough to adapt.

Interactive Element: IEP/504 Plan Preparation Checklist

Creating a checklist can help you stay organized and cover all bases when advocating for your child's IEP or 504 Plan.

1. **Initial Request**

   - Write a formal request to the school
   - Specify concerns and reasons for the request

2. **Evaluation Process**

   - Schedule educational and psychological assessments
   - Gather medical records and teacher observations

3. **Documentation**

   - Collect previous assessments
   - Compile teacher observations and reports

4. **IEP/504 Plan Components**

- Identify specific accommodations needed
- Set measurable goals and objectives
- Determine necessary support services

5. **Advocacy During Meetings**

- Prepare a list of concerns and critical issues
- Bring support (advocate or specialist)
- Keep detailed records of communications and decisions

6. **Ongoing Review**

- Schedule regular reviews and updates
- Adjust accommodations and services as needed

By following this checklist, you can obtain and maintain an effective IEP or 504 Plan for your child, ensuring they receive the support they need to thrive in their educational environment.

BUILDING STRONG RELATIONSHIPS WITH TEACHERS

Building a solid relationship with your child's teacher is crucial for your child's academic success, especially when ADHD is part of the equation. Teachers spend a significant amount of time with your child, often as much as you do, making them pivotal partners in your child's education. Collaboration between parents and teachers ensures everyone works toward the same goals. You create a supportive network around your child by sharing effective strategies and concerns. This teamwork can help address issues before they escalate, making the school experience more positive for everyone involved.

Effective communication is the backbone of a solid parent-teacher relationship. Regular updates are essential. Establish a routine for checking in with the teacher, whether weekly or monthly, to discuss your child's progress and any concerns. This consistency helps maintain an open line of dialogue. Using multiple communication methods can also be beneficial. Emails are great for quick updates, while phone calls or in-person meetings offer more in-depth discussions. Being proactive is vital. Address potential issues as soon as they arise, rather than waiting for them to become significant problems. Apps like Class Dojo can facilitate ongoing communication, providing a platform for sharing updates and tracking progress.

Sharing relevant information about your child can significantly aid the teacher in providing the best support possible. Begin with academic strengths and weaknesses. Highlight areas where your child excels and where they may need extra help. This information helps the teacher tailor their approach, ensuring that your child receives the appropriate level of challenge and support. Behavioral triggers are another essential piece of the puzzle. Identifying specific situations that may cause difficulties allows the teacher to anticipate and manage these challenges effectively. For example, if transitions between activities are particularly hard for your child, the teacher can implement strategies to make these moments smoother.

Discussing effective strategies you've found helpful at home can provide valuable insights for the teacher. If specific techniques work well for managing your child's behavior or improving their focus, share these with the teacher. For instance, if a particular type of positive reinforcement motivates your child, the teacher can incorporate similar approaches in the classroom. This consistency between home and school can create a more stable and predictable environment for your child, making it easier for them to thrive.

Supporting teachers in the classroom is another way to build a strong relationship and ensure your child's success. Resources such as books, articles, and tools on ADHD can be incredibly helpful. Many teachers may not have extensive training in ADHD, so offering these materials can enrich their understanding and provide practical strategies. Volunteering to assist with classroom activities or events is another way to show support. Your presence can reassure your child and provide the teacher with extra hands. Offering constructive feedback can also be beneficial. If you notice something that should be improved, share your observations in a supportive and collaborative manner. This approach fosters mutual respect and a willingness to work together for your child's benefit.

Trust is fundamental to a solid parent-teacher relationship, and trust is built through consistent, honest communication and mutual respect. When teachers see you are actively involved and supportive, they are more likely to reciprocate. Remember, it takes a village to raise a child. Many parents are absent from their child's education, so teachers usually appreciate and welcome parental involvement. Use this to your advantage by being a proactive and engaged partner in your child's education. Show appreciation for the teacher's efforts and acknowledge the challenges they face. A simple thank-you note, or a kind word can go a long way in building a positive rapport.

Visual Element: Communication Log Template

Keeping track of your communications with the teacher can help ensure that essential details are not overlooked. Here's a simple template to use.

1. **Date:**

   - **Method:** (email, phone call, in-person meeting)
   - **Topics Discussed:** (academic progress, behavioral concerns, effective strategies)
   - **Action Items:** (follow-up steps, agreed-upon changes)
   - **Next Check-In Date:**

This template helps you stay organized and ensures all communications are documented and easily accessible.

You can build a strong relationship with your child's teacher by focusing on collaboration, effective communication, and mutual support. This partnership is vital for addressing the unique challenges that come with ADHD and ensuring that your child receives the support they need to succeed academically and socially.

STRATEGIES FOR SUCCESSFUL PARENT-TEACHER MEETINGS

Preparing for a parent-teacher meeting can feel like gearing up for a critical mission. The goal is to ensure the meeting is productive and focused on finding solutions that benefit your child. Start by setting a detailed agenda. List the topics you want to discuss, such as academic progress, behavioral concerns, and specific strategies that have worked at home. Being detailed helps keep the meeting on track and ensures that all important points are covered. Meetings can easily stray off-topic, so having a clear agenda can act as a roadmap, guiding the conversation toward meaningful outcomes.

Gathering documentation is another essential step in preparation. Bring progress reports and behavior logs from school and include your behavior charts and reward logs from home. These documents provide a comprehensive view of your child's performance and behavior, offering valuable insights to help shape the discussion. Showing what has been effective at home can provide a basis for implementing similar strategies in the classroom. This shared understanding can create a cohesive approach that benefits your child in both settings.

Clarifying your goals for the meeting is equally important. Identify the specific outcomes you hope to achieve. Whether getting additional support for your child, addressing a particular behavioral issue, or discussing accommodations, having clear goals ensures the meeting is purposeful. Remember, your role is to be an ally in your child's academic success. If you disagree with the teacher's methods, approach the conversation in a spirit of cooperation. This attitude fosters a positive and productive dialogue, focusing on what's best for your child.

Conducting the meeting effectively requires active listening and clear communication. Pay close attention to what the teacher says, and take notes to help you remember key points and follow up later. Asking specific questions can clarify any concerns and provide a deeper understanding. For example, if the teacher mentions that your child struggles with transitions, ask for specific instances and what strategies have been used. This information can help you work together to find more effective solutions.

Staying focused during the meeting is crucial. It's easy for discussions to drift into generalities or unrelated topics. Refer back to your agenda to keep the conversation on track. If the discussion veers off course, gently steer it back by saying something like, "I'd like to return to the topic of classroom accommodations." This approach keeps the meeting productive and addresses all your key points.

Addressing challenges and concerns can be sensitive, but it's important to approach these discussions constructively. Using "I" statements can help express your concerns without placing blame. For instance, say, "I've noticed that my child seems anxious about homework and often struggles to complete it," rather than, "You give too much homework." This phrasing focuses on the problem without making the teacher feel defensive. Seeking collaborative solutions is the next step. Work together to brainstorm possible strategies and be open to the teacher's suggestions. This collaborative approach often leads to more effective and sustainable solutions.

Staying calm during the discussion is vital. Emotions can run high when discussing your child's struggles, but maintaining composure helps keep the conversation constructive. Take deep breaths and remind yourself that the goal is to support your child's success. If emotions do start to escalate, it's okay to ask for a short break to regroup. This pause can help defuse tension and bring the focus back to finding solutions.

Following up after the meeting is just as important as the meeting itself. Send a follow-up email summarizing the key points discussed and any agreed-upon actions. This recap ensures that everyone is on the same page and provides a written record of the discussion. Setting future check-ins is another necessary step. Schedule the next meeting to review progress and make any necessary adjustments. This ongoing communication helps keep the plan dynamic and responsive to your child's evolving needs.

Monitoring progress is the final piece of the puzzle. Keep track of the agreed-upon actions and note any changes in your child's performance or behavior. Regularly review these notes and bring them to follow-up meetings. This documentation provides a clear picture of what's working and what might need to be adjusted. It also shows that you are actively engaged in your child's education, reinforcing the collaborative partnership with the teacher.

Building a solid relationship with educators and effectively advocating for your child ensures they receive the support they need to thrive. By preparing thoroughly, conducting the meeting effectively, addressing challenges constructively, and following up diligently, you create a supportive network that fosters your child's academic and social success.

ADHD AS AN EVOLUTIONARY ADVANTAGE

Everybody is a genius. But if you judge a fish by its ability to climb a tree, it will live its whole life believing that it is stupid.

— ALBERT EINSTEIN

I recently read an article about how ADHD may have been an evolutionary advantage for our ancestors, their tendency to become distracted and impulsive being helpful when it came to foraging (Davis, 2024). The article pointed to a study in which people played a foraging game online, the goal being to collect the highest number of berries possible in eight minutes. Participants could collect berries from the bushes near them (which would decrease in fruit the more they were foraged) or they could move somewhere else, which took a little more time. Those with ADHD-like symptoms spent less time in a single patch of bushes than those without, moving to new bushes more frequently, and gathering more fruit as a result (Barack et al., 2024).

This idea resonated with me because I've often thought about how I might have experienced my own ADHD in a more positive way if it had had a different environment to fit into. I see this with my own child too; perhaps if fitting into the school environment wasn't so essential, the traits of ADHD could be more easily channeled in ways that allowed them to be helpful. Sadly, though, this is not the world we live in, and the reason why parenting a child with ADHD poses so many challenges is that we need to find ways to help our children function within the structures of modern society. I wrote this book because I recognize this, but I also see the creativity and positive energy that come with an ADHD brain, and I want as many parents as possible to be able to help their children get through life easily and come to view ADHD as a superpower.

Now that you're this far along on our journey together, I'd like to ask for your help in reaching more of those parents—and that's as easy as leaving a short review.

By leaving a review of this book on Amazon, you'll help more parents find the guidance they're looking for and bring balance to their currently chaotic homes.

Reviews help new readers find the information they're looking for, so a few words from you could make a huge difference. I'd love it if ADHD gave our kids the same advantage as it may have given our ancestors, but since we no longer live in the age of the hunter-gatherer, we're going to have to help them instead.

Thank you so much for your support. It's going to make a huge difference to other families.

Scan the QR code below

ADDRESSING COMMON CHALLENGES AT SCHOOL

Imagine your child sitting in a classroom surrounded by peers but struggling to keep up. They squirm in their seat, their eyes darting around the room, distracted by every little noise and movement. For children with ADHD, the classroom can be a minefield of distractions and challenges. As a parent, you want to help your child navigate this environment successfully. Understanding the specific attention-related difficulties they face and knowing how to advocate for effective classroom accommodations can make all the difference.

STRATEGIES FOR FOCUS AND ATTENTION IN THE CLASSROOM

Children with ADHD often face significant challenges in maintaining focus and attention in the classroom. One of the most common difficulties is sustaining attention on tasks for long periods. Your child may start an assignment with good intentions but quickly lose focus as their mind wanders. They may be easily distracted by external stimuli, such as a classmate's whisper, the hum of fluorescent lights, or even the view outside the window. This distractibility can make it nearly impossible for them to stay on task, leading to incomplete assignments and frustration.

Another challenge is task initiation. Your child may know what needs to be done but need help to begin the task. This hesitation can stem from feeling overwhelmed by the complexity of the assignment or simply not knowing where to start. This difficulty can manifest as procrastination, where your child avoids starting their work until the last minute, adding to their stress and anxiety.

You can request several classroom accommodations through an IEP or 504 Plan to support your child in overcoming these challenges. One effective strategy is preferential seating. By sitting your child near the teacher and away from potential distractions, you can help them stay focused on the lesson. This proximity allows the teacher to provide more immediate support and redirection when necessary. Additionally, allowing short, frequent breaks can help manage restlessness. These breaks can be as simple as a quick walk to the water fountain or stretching. They allow your child to release pent-up energy and return to work with renewed focus.

Visual aids can also be beneficial. Charts, diagrams, and other visual tools can help your child better understand and retain information. For example, a visual schedule outlining the day's activities can provide a clear framework, helping your child anticipate what's coming next and stay on track. Classroom fidgets, such as stress balls or small handheld toys, can provide a discreet way for your child to manage their energy and maintain focus. These tools can be beneficial during long periods of instruction or testing.

Teaching self-monitoring techniques is another essential component of supporting your child's focus and attention. Personal task lists can help your child track their assignments and ensure they complete each step. These checklists can be simple, with items to check off as they go, providing a sense of accomplishment and progress. Time management tools like timers and alarms can help your child stay on schedule and manage their time effectively. For instance, setting a timer for fifteen-minute work intervals followed by a short break can make tasks feel more manageable. Self-rating scales, where your child reflects on their focus and behavior, can help them develop greater self-awareness. Encouraging your child to rate their focus level at different points during the day can provide valuable insights and help them identify patterns and triggers.

Ongoing communication and collaboration with teachers are crucial for consistently implementing focus strategies. Regular meetings with teachers allow for open dialogue about your child's progress and any adjustments that may be needed. These check-ins can also provide an opportunity to share what's working at home and discuss how your strategies can be adapted for the classroom. Progress reports can update your child's attention and behavior, helping you stay informed and involved in their education. Providing resources to help teachers understand ADHD can also be beneficial. Sharing articles and books or inviting experts to speak at school can help educators better understand ADHD and its impact on learning.

Interactive Element: Focus and Attention Checklist

Creating a checklist can help you and your child stay on top of the strategies discussed. Here's an example.

1. **Preferential Seating**

   - **Task:** Sit near the teacher and away from distractions.
   - **Goal:** Improve focus and reduce distractions.

2. **Breaks**

   - **Task:** Take short, frequent breaks.
   - **Goal:** Manage restlessness and maintain focus.

3. **Visual Aids**

   - **Task:** Use charts and visuals to aid comprehension.
   - **Goal:** Enhance understanding and retention of information.

4. **Classroom Fidgets**

   - **Task:** Use stress balls or small handheld toys.
   - **Goal:** Manage energy and maintain focus.

5. **Self-Monitoring Techniques**

   - **Task:** Use checklists, timers, and self-rating scales.
   - **Goal:** Develop self-awareness and improve time management.

6. **Collaboration with Teachers**

   - **Task:** Schedule regular meetings and share progress reports.
   - **Goal:** Ensure consistent implementation of focus strategies.

By identifying common attention challenges, implementing classroom accommodations, teaching self-monitoring techniques, and fostering collaboration with teachers, you can help your child navigate the classroom more effectively. These strategies provide a comprehensive approach to supporting your child's focus and attention, helping them thrive in their educational environment.

HOMEWORK HELP: MAKING AFTER-SCHOOL TIME PRODUCTIVE

Creating a structured homework routine is a cornerstone for making after-school time productive and stress-free for your child. Consistency is key here. Establishing a scheduled homework time that occurs at a particular time each day can do wonders. This predictable routine helps your child anticipate what's coming next, reducing anxiety and resistance. Breaks and rewards are vital components of this routine. Incorporate short rest periods between work sessions, allowing your child to recharge. For example, a five-minute break after ten to fifteen minutes of focused work can help maintain concentration. Pair these breaks with small rewards to keep them motivated. Clear expectations are also essential. Set specific homework goals for each session so your child knows exactly what needs to be accomplished before they move on. This clarity can help them focus and reduce the feeling of being overwhelmed.

Setting up an effective homework environment can significantly affect your child's ability to focus and complete their assignments. Start by designating a dedicated homework area that is quiet and organized. This space should be free from distractions like toys, gadgets, or noisy siblings. Keeping essential supplies within reach is equally important. Ensure that pencils, paper, calculators, and other necessary materials are readily available. This setup minimizes the need for your child to get up frequently, which can easily lead to distractions. Limiting distractions extends beyond the physical setup. Reducing noise and visual clutter in the homework area can create a calm and focused environment. Consider using noise-canceling headphones or playing soft background music to drown out household noises. Keeping the workspace tidy and free of unnecessary items can also help your child concentrate better.

Homework strategies that enhance focus and understanding are essential. One effective method is chunking tasks. Breaking assignments into smaller, manageable parts can make the workload seem less daunting. If your child attends an after-school program, see if they offer homework help. Have your child do some homework there, dividing the tasks into smaller chunks. Active learning techniques can also be beneficial. Hands-on activities and visual aids can make learning more engaging and easier to understand. For instance, using flashcards or drawing diagrams can help reinforce concepts. Homework planners are invaluable tools for tracking assignments and deadlines. Encourage your child to use a planner to track what needs to be accomplished and when. Introducing methods like the Critical Path Method or Gantt charts can teach them to prioritize tasks and manage their time effectively.

Addressing common homework challenges is crucial for maintaining a productive and positive after-school routine. Procrastination is a common issue for children with ADHD. This technique, known as the Pomodoro Technique, can make tasks more manageable and less overwhelming. Frustration is another hurdle. Encourage your child to take breaks when frustrated and offer assistance as needed. Sometimes, redirecting their attention to non-homework tasks that need to be done and then coming back to the homework can help reset their focus. Lack of motivation can be addressed through positive reinforcement and rewards. Explain to your child how completing their homework now will free up more time for activities they enjoy later. This connection between effort and reward can boost their motivation and make the task feel more worthwhile.

Creating a structured homework routine, setting up an effective homework environment, using specific strategies to enhance focus, and addressing common homework challenges can transform after-school time from chaotic to productive. These steps provide a clear framework that helps your child navigate their homework with greater ease and confidence. By incorporating breaks, rewards, and techniques tailored to their needs, you can support your child in developing the skills and habits necessary for academic success.

HANDLING BULLYING AND SOCIAL ISSUES AT SCHOOL

Recognizing the signs of bullying in children with ADHD is crucial, as they are often more vulnerable to being targeted. Behavioral changes can be a red flag. A child who was once outgoing and enthusiastic may suddenly become withdrawn and quiet. Alternatively, they may exhibit increased aggression, lashing out at peers or family members. These shifts in behavior can indicate that something is wrong and should not be dismissed as mere mood swings. Physical signs are also telling. Unexplained injuries, like bruises or scratches, can be a clear indicator of physical bullying. Similarly, if your child frequently comes home with damaged belongings, such as torn clothes or broken school supplies, it might be a sign that they are being targeted. Additionally, an unexpected decline in academic performance or a sudden lack of interest in school activities can signal emotional distress. If your child, who once enjoyed going to school, starts making excuses to stay home, it's time to dig deeper.

It's important to teach children how to respond to bullying. Start with assertiveness training. Encourage your child to practice confident responses. Role-playing scenarios at home can help them develop the skills to stand up for themselves without resorting to aggression. Teach them simple, firm phrases like, "Stop that, it's not okay," or "Leave me alone." These assertive statements can empower your child to take control of the situation. Equally important is knowing when and how to seek help. Ensure your child understands it's okay to report bullying to a trusted adult, whether a teacher, school counselor, or you. Reinforce that asking for help is not a sign of weakness but a courageous step toward resolving the issue. Building resilience is another key aspect. Focus on encouraging your child's self-esteem and confidence. Praise their strengths and achievements, no matter how small. Activities that promote self-worth, like sports, arts, or hobbies, can also be incredibly beneficial. These activities provide a sense of accomplishment and opportunities to build new friendships and provide creative and social outlets.

Working with the school to address bullying is vital. Start by understanding the school's reporting procedures. Document any bullying incidents, including dates, times, and descriptions of what happened. This documentation will be invaluable when discussing the issue with school staff. Familiarize yourself with the school's anti-bullying policies and procedures. Knowing these policies can empower you to advocate effectively for your child. Engage the support staff, such as school counselors and psychologists. These professionals can provide additional resources and support for your child. Collaborate with them to develop a plan that addresses the bullying and supports your child's emotional well-being.

Supporting your child emotionally during this time is critical. Open communication is the foundation. Encourage your child to talk about their experiences without fear of judgment. Create a safe space where they feel heard and understood. Emotional validation is equally essential. Acknowledge their feelings and let them know feeling scared, angry, or sad is okay. Validating their emotions can help them process their experiences and feel less isolated. Teaching relaxation and stress management techniques can also be beneficial. Simple practices like deep breathing, progressive muscle relaxation, or mindfulness can help your child manage their emotions and reduce anxiety. These coping strategies can provide them with tools to navigate stressful situations at school and other areas of their life.

As you navigate these challenges, remember that your support and understanding are invaluable. By recognizing the signs of bullying, teaching your child how to respond assertively, working with the school, and providing emotional support, you can help your child build resilience and navigate social issues more confidently. These steps create a foundation for a safer and more supportive school environment where your child can focus on learning and growing.

HOLISTIC APPROACHES TO ADHD MANAGEMENT

Imagine your child's body as a finely tuned engine. Just like an engine needs the right fuel to run smoothly, your child's brain and body require the proper nutrients to function optimally. Nutrition plays a crucial role in managing ADHD symptoms. You may have noticed that certain foods calm your child while others make them bounce off the walls. This chapter delves into how diet can impact ADHD, offering practical advice on what to include and avoid in your child's meals.

NUTRITION AND ADHD: FOODS THAT HELP

The link between diet and ADHD symptoms is not just anecdotal; it's backed by research. Nutritional deficiencies can significantly impact brain function and behavior. For instance, a lack of essential nutrients can lead to imbalances in neurotransmitters, the chemicals responsible for transmitting signals in the brain. These imbalances can exacerbate symptoms like inattention, hyperactivity, and impulsivity. Blood sugar levels also play a significant role. When blood sugar spikes and crashes, it can lead to fluctuations in energy and focus. This rollercoaster effect can make it difficult for your child to maintain steady attention and control impulses.

Certain nutrients have been shown to support brain health and improve ADHD symptoms. Omega-3 fatty acids, for instance, are essential for brain function. These healthy fats are found in fish like salmon and mackerel, as well as in flaxseeds and walnuts. Omega-3s help to build cell membranes in the brain, promoting better communication between neurons. Protein is another crucial nutrient. Protein is found in lean meats, eggs, beans, nuts, and dairy products, providing building blocks for neurotransmitters. Including a source of protein in your child's breakfast can help stabilize blood sugar levels and improve focus throughout the morning. Complex carbohydrates from whole grains, fruits, and vegetables provide a steady release of energy, avoiding the spikes and crashes associated with simple sugars.

Incorporating ADHD-friendly foods into your child's diet can be nutritious and delicious. Fatty fish like salmon and mackerel are excellent sources of omega-3 fatty acids. Grilling salmon with a simple lemon and herb marinade would make it tasty and kid-friendly. Leafy greens like spinach and kale are packed with essential vitamins and minerals. For a nutrient-rich breakfast, you can blend them into smoothies with your child's favorite fruits. Nuts and seeds, like almonds, chia seeds, cashews, and pistachios, make healthy snacks packed with plant-based protein. They are rich in healthy fats and provide kids with a satisfying crunch. Whole grains like oatmeal, quinoa, and granola offer sustained energy. Consider preparing a warm bowl of oatmeal topped with fresh fruit and a sprinkle of nuts for a balanced meal. Kid not a fan of oatmeal? Try granola with honey and milk topped with berries. Fresh fruits like apples, pears, peaches, plums, and nectarines are naturally sweet and packed with vitamins.

While it's essential to focus on what to include in your child's diet, it's equally crucial to be mindful of what to avoid. Sugary snacks, such as candies and sodas, can lead to rapid spikes and crashes in blood sugar levels, exacerbating hyperactivity and inattention. Artificial additives, including food colorings and preservatives, have been linked to increased hyperactivity in some children. Processed foods, often laden with unhealthy fats and sugars, lack the essential nutrients for optimal brain function. Fast food and packaged snacks should be limited, as they can contribute to nutritional imbalances and make ADHD symptoms worse.

Creating a meal plan that supports your child's ADHD can be a rewarding endeavor. Start by incorporating more beneficial nutrients and ADHD-friendly foods into your meals. Gradually reduce the intake of sugary snacks, artificial additives, and processed foods. This balanced approach can help stabilize your child's energy levels, focus, and overall well-being.

Interactive Element: ADHD-Friendly Meal Planner

Creating a meal planner can help you incorporate these ADHD-friendly foods into your child's diet. Here's an example:

Breakfast:

- **Option 1:** Oatmeal topped with fresh fruit and nuts
- **Option 2:** Smoothie with leafy greens, berries, and chia seeds
- **Option 3:** Granola with milk and honey topped with berries

Lunch:

- **Option 1:** Grilled salmon with quinoa and steamed vegetables
- **Option 2:** Lean turkey sandwich on whole grain bread with a side of pear slices
- **Option 3**: Lean un-breaded chicken nuggets with kale chips and low-sugar yogurt

Snacks:

- **Option 1:** A handful of almonds and a piece of fresh fruit
- **Option 2:** Greek yogurt with granola and a drizzle of honey
- **Option 3**: vegetable/fruit puree packs with some dehydrated fruit or veggie chips

Dinner:

- **Option 1:** Baked Chicken with roasted sweet potatoes and a mixed greens salad
- **Option 2:** Beef stir-fry with a variety of colorful vegetables and brown rice
- **Option 3:** Lean pork chop with apple chutney or glaze and a side of oven-charred broccoli or squash

Foods to Avoid:

- **Sugary Snacks:** Candies, sodas
- **Artificial Additives:** Food colorings, preservatives
- **Processed Foods:** Fast food, frozen foods with long ingredients lists

Focusing on a balanced diet rich in essential nutrients and being mindful of foods exacerbating symptoms can create a supportive nutritional environment for your child. This holistic approach to managing ADHD through nutrition can make a significant difference in their daily lives, enhancing their ability to focus, stay calm, and perform at their best.

EXERCISE ROUTINES TO BOOST FOCUS AND ENERGY

Regular physical activity is a powerful tool for managing ADHD symptoms. Exercise can improve focus, reduce hyperactivity, and enhance overall mental health for children with ADHD. When your child engages in physical activity, their brain releases dopamine and norepinephrine, neurotransmitters that play a crucial role in attention and behavior regulation. These chemicals help improve brain function, making it easier for your child to stay focused and attentive. Additionally, exercise helps lower cortisol levels, the hormone associated with stress. Reducing cortisol can decrease anxiety and promote a sense of calm. Physical activity also aids in balancing energy levels, helping to regulate both hyperactivity and lethargy. This balance ensures your child has enough energy to stay engaged throughout the day without becoming restless or sleepy.

Certain types of exercise are particularly beneficial. Aerobic exercises like running, swimming, and cycling are excellent choices. These activities increase heart rate and promote cardiovascular health, improving oxygen flow to the brain. This boost in oxygen can enhance cognitive function and concentration. Imagine your child running through the park, feeling the wind on their face, and using up their boundless energy productively. Swimming offers a full-body workout that's both fun and calming. The rhythmic movement and the sensation of water can be soothing for children with ADHD. Cycling around the neighborhood or on a stationary bike provides a great way to get the heart pumping and the brain engaged.

Strength training is another effective form of exercise. Body-weight exercises like push-ups, squats, and planks can help build muscle strength and improve overall fitness. Resistance bands are also a helpful tool for strength training. These bands are versatile and can be used to target different muscle groups. Strength training not only builds physical strength but also enhances mental resilience. The discipline and focus required to perform these exercises can translate to better concentration and self-control in other areas of life.

Mind-body exercises like yoga and tai chi offer unique benefits. Yoga combines physical postures with breathing exercises and meditation, promoting balance and calm. It helps improve flexibility, strength, and focus. Imagine your child practicing yoga, moving through poses like the tree pose or downward dog, and learning to control their breath. These exercises teach mindfulness, helping your child become more aware of their thoughts and actions. Tai chi, a form of martial arts, involves slow, deliberate movements and deep breathing. This practice can enhance coordination, balance, and relaxation, making it an excellent option for children with ADHD.

Creating a balanced exercise routine ensures that your child stays engaged and reaps the benefits of different types of physical activity. A daily schedule that allocates time for various exercises can be highly effective. For example, start the day with a fifteen-minute yoga session to promote calm and focus. Mid-morning, incorporate thirty minutes of aerobic activity like running or cycling to boost energy levels. In the afternoon, include a twenty-minute strength training session using body-weight exercises or resistance bands. Mixing high-intensity and low-intensity exercises keeps the routine exciting and prevents burnout. Including fun activities like sports and games can make exercise enjoyable. Encourage your child to participate in team sports like soccer or basketball, which promote physical fitness and social skills.

Integrating physical activity into daily life doesn't have to be a chore. Encourage active play by setting up outdoor games and sports. A simple game of tag or a session of catch can provide a great workout. Family activities like hiking, biking, or dancing together can make exercise a bonding experience. Take your dog for a walk, go on a family bike ride, or have a dance party in the living room. These activities not only promote physical fitness but also create lasting memories. School involvement is another avenue to explore. Ensure your child participates in PE classes and encourage them to join sports teams or clubs. These structured activities provide regular opportunities for exercise and help your child develop discipline and teamwork skills.

Physical activity is a vital component of managing ADHD symptoms. Incorporating regular exercise into your child's routine can help improve their focus, reduce hyperactivity, and enhance their overall mental health. Whether through aerobic workouts, strength training, or mind-body practices, the benefits of physical activity are profound. Creating a balanced exercise routine and integrating movement into daily life can make a significant difference in your child's ability to manage ADHD and thrive.

SLEEP HYGIENE: ENSURING RESTFUL NIGHTS

Good sleep is a cornerstone for children with ADHD. Quality sleep impacts brain function, emotional regulation, and physical health. When your child sleeps well, their cognitive performance improves, enabling them to focus better and retain information more effectively. You might notice that when they sleep poorly, their inattention and hyperactivity seem magnified. This isn't a coincidence. Sleep plays a crucial role in how well their brain can process and store information.

Emotional regulation is another area significantly influenced by sleep. Well-rested children are better equipped to manage their emotions. You may find that your child is less prone to emotional outbursts and mood swings after a good night's sleep. This stability is essential for their overall well-being and helps create a more harmonious home environment. Physical health is also directly tied to sleep. During sleep, the body undergoes crucial processes that support growth and development. For a growing child, adequate sleep helps them reach their full physical potential.

Establishing a consistent sleep routine is critical to ensuring your child gets the restful sleep they need. Start by setting a regular sleep schedule. Have a consistent bedtime and wake-up time, even on weekends. A regular schedule helps regulate your child's internal clock, making it easier for them to fall asleep and wake up naturally. Pre-bedtime activities should be calming and help signal to your child that it's time to wind down. Reading a book together or listening to soft music can be soothing and set the stage for sleep. Avoid stimulating activities like watching TV or playing video games right before bed, as these can make it harder for your child to settle down.

Another essential step is creating an optimal sleep environment. The bedroom should be dark, quiet, and cool. Consider using blackout curtains to block light and a white noise machine to drown out disruptive sounds. These simple adjustments can make a significant difference in helping your child fall asleep and stay asleep. The proper sleep environment can create a sanctuary of calm, making it easier for your child to relax and drift off.

Many children with ADHD face sleep challenges, such as difficulty falling asleep, frequent awakening, and restless sleep. Relaxation techniques can be highly effective in addressing these issues. Teach your child deep breathing exercises, in which they take slow, deep breaths to calm their mind and body. Progressive muscle relaxation, in which they tense and then relax different muscle groups, can also help release physical tension. Limiting screen time before bed is critical. The blue light emitted by screens can interfere with the production of melatonin, a hormone that regulates sleep. Encourage your child to avoid electronics at least an hour before bedtime.

Comfort items can also significantly improve sleep quality. Weighted blankets provide gentle, soothing pressure and help your child feel more secure. White noise machines can create a consistent sound environment that masks other noises and helps your child stay asleep. These tools can become part of your child's bedtime routine, making the transition to sleep smoother and more comfortable.

Monitoring and improving sleep quality is an ongoing process. Keeping a sleep diary can be an effective way to track your child's sleep patterns and behaviors. Record when they go to bed, how long it takes to fall asleep, any awakenings during the night, and what time they wake up. This information can help identify patterns and areas that need improvement. Sleep trackers, such as wearable devices or apps, can provide additional insights into your child's sleep. These tools can monitor factors like sleep duration and quality, providing a more detailed picture of their sleep habits. If sleep issues persist, consulting a sleep specialist may be necessary. A professional can offer tailored advice and interventions to help your child achieve better sleep.

Sleep hygiene is a vital aspect of managing ADHD. Focusing on quality sleep can significantly improve your child's cognitive performance, emotional stability, and physical health. Establishing a consistent sleep routine, creating an optimal sleep environment, addressing common sleep challenges, and monitoring sleep quality are all essential steps in promoting restful nights for your child.

In the next chapter, we will explore the empowering aspects of ADHD, with a focus on discovering and nurturing your child's unique strengths. This journey is about managing symptoms and helping your child thrive in every aspect of their life.

EMPOWERING YOUR ADHD CHILD

~~~

Imagine your child as a budding artist, each brushstroke a unique talent waiting to be discovered and nurtured. As parents of children with ADHD, you have the opportunity to help your child uncover their hidden strengths and superpowers! While ADHD often comes with challenges, it also brings unique perspectives and capabilities. When we foster our children's strengths and mitigate their challenges it can lead to extraordinary achievements. This chapter focuses on discovering and nurturing your child's strengths, turning them into well-honed skills that will empower them throughout their lives.

DISCOVERING AND NURTURING YOUR CHILD'S STRENGTHS

Recognizing and celebrating your child's unique strengths and talents is crucial for their self-esteem and overall development. Each child possesses strengths that can become powerful assets when identified and nurtured. To start, consider using tools like StrengthsFinder for Kids. This assessment helps pinpoint specific talents, clearly showing where your child excels. It's an invaluable resource to help you understand your child's natural abilities.

Observing your child's interests is another effective way to identify their strengths. Pay attention to the activities they are naturally drawn to and excited about. Whether building intricate structures with LEGO, creating detailed drawings, or showing an interest in science experiments, these activities can reveal innate talents. Encourage your child to explore these interests further, as they often provide a window into their strengths.

Feedback from others, such as teachers and friends, can also offer valuable insights. Teachers, in particular, spend a significant amount of time with your child in a structured environment and can identify strengths that may not be as evident at home. Friends can provide a different perspective, noting qualities like leadership, creativity, or empathy that your child exhibits in social settings. This collective feedback helps paint a comprehensive picture of your child's strengths.

Fostering an environment that encourages exploration and curiosity is key to helping your child develop their talents. Provide resources that cater to their interests, such as books, kits, and materials. For instance, if your child is interested in astronomy, consider getting them a beginner's telescope and books about space. Encouraging questions and supporting their curiosity can lead to deeper exploration and learning. Create a space where your child feels comfortable asking questions and exploring new topics without fear of judgment.

Enrolling your child in clubs, classes, or workshops can also be beneficial. These activities provide structured environments where your child can dive deeper into their interests and develop their skills. For example, a child interested in music may thrive in a local music class where they can learn to play an instrument.

Trying new activities can open new avenues for discovering hidden talents and passions.

Once you have identified your child's strengths, the next step is to support and develop them. Skill-building activities, such as practice sessions or structured lessons, can help turn these strengths into well-honed skills. For instance, if your child shows a talent for writing, encourage regular writing practice and consider enrolling them in a creative writing class. Structured lessons provide a framework for developing skills in a focused and consistent manner.

Finding a mentor in your child's area of interest can also be incredibly beneficial. A mentor can provide guidance, share their experiences, and offer valuable insights to help your child navigate their interests. This relationship can inspire your child and provide them with a role model to look up to. Celebrating your child's progress and achievements is equally important. Highlight improvements and accomplishments, no matter how small, to boost their confidence and motivation.

Integrating your child's strengths into their daily routines and responsibilities can make them feel more competent and valued. Assigning strength-based chores is one way to do this. For example if the child enjoys interacting with the family pet assign them tasks that nurtures that joy, even if the tasks surrounding pet care aren't much fun. This uses their strengths and fosters a sense of responsibility and contribution.

Encourage your child to incorporate their strengths into school projects. If they have a talent for art, suggest they create visual presentations or posters for their assignments. Artistic expression allows them to shine in their areas of strength while also fulfilling academic requirements. Planning family activities around your child's strengths can also be a fantastic way to celebrate and nurture their talents. For instance, if your child loves cooking, involve them in planning and preparing family meals. Involvement in this task reinforces their skills and strengthens family bonds.

By recognizing, celebrating, and nurturing your child's strengths, you empower them to thrive. Turn these talents into well-honed skills and integrate them into daily life, making your child feel competent and valued. Encourage exploration and curiosity, provide resources, and seek feedback from teachers and friends. Support their interests through clubs, classes, and mentorship, celebrating their progress along the way. By doing so, you help your child build a strong foundation for future success, transforming challenges into opportunities for growth and achievement.

SUCCESS STORIES: INSPIRING EXAMPLES OF ADHD BRILLIANCE

Real-life success stories can be incredibly motivating, especially when they highlight the unique strengths and talents of individuals with ADHD. Take, for example, Richard Branson, the founder of the Virgin Group. Branson was diagnosed with ADHD and has built a business empire that spans various industries. His ability to think creatively and take risks has been a significant factor in his success. Branson often credits his ADHD with giving him the energy and drive needed to overcome obstacles and innovate in ways others might not consider. His story shows that ADHD can be a powerful asset in the world of entrepreneurship.

In the realm of sports and physicality, ADHD has also played a pivotal role. Consider the case of Michael Phelps, the most decorated Olympian ever. Phelps was diagnosed with ADHD at a young age, and he faced challenges both in school and in his early swimming career. However, he learned to channel his hyperfocus into his training, using it to achieve remarkable feats in swimming. His story illustrates how intense focus, a common trait in those with ADHD, can be harnessed to achieve extraordinary goals. Phelps' success is a testament to how ADHD can become a source of strength and resilience when managed well.

The scientific community is not without its share of ADHD success stories. Dr. Edward Hallowell, a renowned psychiatrist and ADHD expert, has made groundbreaking contributions to our understanding of the condition. Diagnosed with ADHD himself, Dr. Hallowell has used his personal experiences to inform his work, helping countless individuals navigate their ADHD successfully. His ability to think outside the box and approach problems from unique angles has been instrumental in his success. Dr. Hallowell's story underscores the importance of leveraging creativity and resilience, traits often found in individuals with ADHD, in achieving one's goals.

Another athlete who has made significant strides is Simone Biles, one of the greatest gymnasts of all time. She has openly discussed her ADHD diagnosis. Biles has used her condition to her advantage, channeling her abundant energy and focus into her rigorous training regime. Her success in gymnastics demonstrates how ADHD traits can be effectively managed and used to excel in sports. Biles' story is a powerful reminder that ADHD is not a barrier to success but rather a different way of experiencing and interacting with the world.

When we analyze these success stories, several common traits emerge. Resilience is a crucial factor. Individuals with ADHD often face setbacks, but their ability to bounce back and persevere is remarkable. This resilience is not just about enduring challenges but also about learning from them and growing stronger. Creativity is another common trait. People with ADHD frequently think outside the box, creating innovative solutions to problems. This ability to see things from unique perspectives can be a significant advantage in various fields.

Another important trait is hyperfocus. While ADHD is often associated with difficulties maintaining attention, it also comes with the ability to focus intensely on tasks that are engaging or stimulating. When channeled effectively, this hyperfocus can lead to exceptional achievements. Hyperfocus has its drawbacks and may be a double-edged sword when it strays into obsessive territory. Adaptability is crucial. Individuals with ADHD often thrive in dynamic environments where they can use their adaptability to navigate changing circumstances and seize new opportunities.

Creating a supportive environment is essential for fostering success in children with ADHD. Encouraging mentors can play a pivotal role in this process. Mentors provide guidance, share their experiences, and offer valuable insights to help your child navigate their interests and challenges. Supportive peers are equally important. Friends and colleagues who understand and encourage your child can create a positive and motivating environment. Flexible structures, such as adaptable routines and expectations, can help your child manage their ADHD traits effectively and thrive.

Encouraging goal-setting and aspirations can further empower your child. Vision boards are an excellent tool for visualizing and planning future achievements. By creating a vision board, your child can map out their goals and dreams, making them more tangible and attainable. Setting SMART goals—Specific, Measurable, Achievable, Relevant, and Time-bound—can provide a clear framework for achieving these aspirations. Regular check-ins to monitor progress and adjust plans as needed can keep your child on track and motivated.

Interactive Element: Vision Board Activity

Creating a vision board can be a fun and inspiring activity for you and your child. Gather magazines, scissors, glue, and a large poster board. Ask your child to cut out images and words representing their goals and dreams. Arrange these on the poster board in a visually appealing way. Hang the vision board where your child can see it daily. This visual reminder can keep them focused on their aspirations and motivated to achieve them.

By sharing inspiring success stories, analyzing common success traits, and highlighting the importance of a supportive environment, you can help your child see the potential that lies within them. Encouraging goal-setting and aspirations can further empower them, turning their ADHD traits into powerful assets for future success.

BUILDING SELF-ESTEEM AND CONFIDENCE

Understanding the importance of self-esteem is crucial when raising a child with ADHD. Self-esteem and confidence are the bedrock upon which your child's emotional and social well-being are built. They impact how your child handles challenges and setbacks, interacts with peers, and performs academically. When children believe in their abilities, they are more likely to take risks, try new things, and persist in the face of difficulties. Emotional resilience, which is the ability to bounce back from setbacks, is nurtured by a strong sense of self-worth. This resilience is essential for children with ADHD, as they often face more challenges than their peers do. Confidence helps them build positive relationships and navigate complexities in social interactions. Academically, increased self-esteem translates to higher motivation and persistence, leading to better performance and a more positive attitude toward learning.

Providing positive reinforcement and encouragement is one of the most effective ways to boost your child's self-esteem. Praise efforts rather than just results. Recognize your child's hard work and persistence in tasks, even if the outcome isn't perfect. This kind of praise encourages a growth mindset, which means your child learns to see challenges as opportunities for growth rather than insurmountable obstacles. Celebrate achievements, both big and small. Whether it's a good grade on a test or completing a challenging project, acknowledging these successes reinforces your child's belief in their abilities. Use positive language consistently. Words have power, and affirming and supportive words can significantly affect how your child perceives themself. Instead of focusing on what they can't do, highlight what they can and have done well.

Teaching self-advocacy skills is another vital component of building confidence. Children with ADHD often need to advocate for themselves in various settings, such as school, social situations, and even at home. Role-playing scenarios can be an effective way to practice self-advocacy. Create scenarios in which your child may need to speak up for themselves, such as asking a teacher for extra help or explaining their needs to a friend. This practice can build their confidence and prepare them for real-life situations. Encouraging self-expression is also essential. Help your child articulate their needs and preferences clearly and confidently. Try teaching them specific phrases or strategies for communicating their needs. Providing tools and resources, such as books or workshops on self-advocacy, can further empower your child. These resources can offer practical advice and techniques, making self-advocacy a more manageable and less intimidating task.

Creating opportunities for success is essential for building self-esteem. Set achievable tasks for your child, gradually increasing the complexity as they become more confident. Start with small, manageable tasks they can complete successfully, then gradually introduce more challenging, multi-step tasks. This approach helps build a sense of competence and accomplishment. Encourage your child to join extracurricular activities that align with their interests and strengths. Whether it's a sports team, a music class, or a science club, these activities allow your child to excel and build confidence in a structured and supportive environment. Leadership roles can also be incredibly empowering. Encourage your child to take on leadership positions, whether being a team captain, a class representative, or leading a group project. These roles can help them develop leadership skills and build confidence in their abilities.

In summary, building self-esteem and confidence involves understanding their unique needs, providing positive reinforcement, teaching self-advocacy skills, and creating opportunities for success. By focusing on these areas, you can help your child develop a strong sense of self-worth, emotional resilience, and the confidence to navigate their world successfully. This chapter highlights the importance of self-esteem in overall well-being and success, emphasizing practical strategies for parents to implement.

NAVIGATING PUBLIC SPACES AND SOCIAL SITUATIONS

Imagine planning a family outing while being filled with excitement and anticipation but also a tinge of anxiety. You know that public spaces can present unique challenges for your child. The unpredictability of these environments can trigger stress, making it crucial to plan meticulously. Preparing for outings requires more than just packing a bag; it involves foreseeing potential obstacles and equipping yourself with strategies to manage them. This chapter is designed to help you anticipate and address your child's unique needs, ensuring that your outings are enjoyable and stress-free for everyone involved.

PREPARING FOR OUTINGS: WHAT TO PACK AND PLAN

The importance of planning cannot be overstated when it comes to outings with a child who has ADHD. Knowing what to expect can significantly reduce surprises and stress. Start by researching your destination thoroughly. Understand the layout, the facilities available, and any potential triggers that could cause discomfort for your child. Whether it's a visit to a museum, a day at the park, or a trip to the zoo, having a clear picture of what the day entails helps prepare you and your child.

Creating a schedule for the day's activities is another essential step. It doesn't have to be written down or formal, but set the expectations early with your child, especially when it comes to when you will be leaving the outing. Verbally communicate the timeline of events, including travel time, meal breaks, rest periods, and end times. Setting expectations about behavior and rules is also important. Discuss appropriate behavior in different settings, such as staying close in crowded areas, using an inside voice, keeping our hands to ourselves, and waiting patiently in lines. This conversation helps your child understand what is expected of them and reduces anxiety about the unknown.

Packing essential items for managing ADHD symptoms can make a significant difference in how smoothly the day goes. Fidget toys like stress balls or spinners can provide a much-needed outlet for restless energy. Healthy, low-sugar snacks help maintain stable blood sugar levels, preventing energy spikes and crashes. Always carry water to keep your child hydrated, as dehydration can exacerbate ADHD symptoms. Comfort items like a favorite blanket or stuffed animal can offer a sense of security and familiarity in unfamiliar settings.

Addressing sensory needs is another critical aspect of preparation. Public spaces can be overwhelming with their myriad sounds, lights, and textures. Noise-cancelling headphones can help manage loud environments, allowing your child to focus and stay calm. Sunglasses or hats can reduce light sensitivity, making bright, sunny days or fluorescent-lit indoor spaces more tolerable. Sensory-friendly clothing, which is comfortable and non-restrictive, can prevent discomfort and distractions caused by tags, seams, or tight fabrics.

Developing a contingency plan is vital for managing unexpected situations. Identify quiet spots where your child can take a break if they become overwhelmed. Places like libraries, benches in a park, or even a calm restaurant corner can serve as temporary retreats. Having an exit strategy is also essential. Know when and how to leave early if the situation becomes unmanageable. Having the car parked nearby or knowing the quickest route to a quieter area will help.

Outing Preparation Checklist

1. **Researching the Destination**

    - Understand the layout and facilities.
    - Identify potential triggers (e.g., loud noises, crowded areas).

2. **Creating a Schedule**

    - Plan the day's activities, including travel time and breaks.
    - Share the schedule with your child and discuss expectations.

3. **Setting Expectations**

    - Discuss appropriate behavior (e.g., staying close, using an inside voice).
    - Explain the rules for different settings.

4. **Packing Essential Items**

    - Snacks: Healthy, low-sugar options.
    - Water: To stay hydrated.

- Comfort items: Favorite blanket, stuffed animal, or small toy.

5. **Preparing for Sensory Needs**

- Noise-cancelling headphones: For loud environments.
- Sunglasses or hats: Reducing light sensitivity.
- Sensory-friendly clothing: Comfortable, non-restrictive attire.

6. **Developing a Contingency Plan**

- Identifying quiet spots: Places to take a break if overwhelmed.
- Exit strategy: Knowing when and how to leave early.

By taking these steps, you create a structured and supportive environment to help your child navigate the complexities of public spaces. This preparation makes the outing more enjoyable and empowers your child to manage their ADHD symptoms more effectively.

HANDLING MELTDOWNS IN PUBLIC

Recognizing the early signs of a meltdown can make all the difference when you're in public with your child. These signs are often subtle but critical indicators that your child is becoming overwhelmed. Increased agitation is one of the first things you'll notice. Your child may start fidgeting more than usual or begin pacing back and forth. These physical manifestations are their way of trying to cope with the overwhelming stimuli around them. Verbal cues are another red flag. Complaints may become more frequent, and their voice may rise in volume. Finally, physical symptoms like a flushed face or rapid breathing indicate your child is nearing their breaking point. By recognizing these early signs, you can intervene before the situation escalates into a full-blown meltdown.

Calming techniques at the first sign of distress can help your child regain control. Deep breathing exercises are a simple yet effective method. Guide your child through the process by encouraging them to take slow, deep breaths. Some apps will help your child visualize the box breathing technique with visual cues on inhale, hold, and exhale. This helps lower their heart rate and gives them something to focus on besides their distress. Distraction is another useful tactic. Redirect their attention to a different activity or object. Try pointing out an interesting feature in your surroundings or engaging them in a quick game. Sensory tools like sensory toys or comfort items can also be beneficial. These items provide a tactile distraction to help soothe your child and redirect their focus.

Creating a calm-down space in public settings is essential for managing meltdowns. Identifying quiet areas where your child can take a break is a good start. Libraries, benches in a park, or even a quiet corner in a restaurant can serve as temporary havens. If you're near your car, that can also act as a familiar and controlled environment where your child can reset. A portable calm-down kit can be a lifesaver in these situations—items like coloring books, earplugs, or a favorite toy can provide the distraction and comfort your child needs to regain their composure.

Communicating effectively during a meltdown is crucial. A calm voice helps soothe your child and lets them know you are there for them. Speak softly and reassuringly, making it clear that you understand their feelings. Offering choices can give your child a sense of control, which is often what they crave during a meltdown. Simple options like, "Would you like to sit here or over there?" can make a big difference. Positive reinforcement is another crucial strategy. Praise your child for any effort they make to calm down, no matter how small. Positive reinforcement helps to de-escalate the situation and encourages them to use these coping mechanisms in the future.

NAVIGATING SOCIAL GATHERINGS AND EVENTS

Social gatherings can be a mixed bag for children with ADHD. The excitement of being around friends and family can quickly turn into anxiety if they're unprepared. Preparing your child for social situations is essential for reducing this anxiety and helping them handle interactions more smoothly. Start by discussing the event with your child. Explain what will happen, who will be there, and what activities might take place. Set clear expectations and remove some uncertainties that can cause anxiety.

Role-playing scenarios can be an effective way to prepare. Have your child practice everyday social interactions they may encounter, such as greeting someone or joining a group activity. This rehearsal gives your child the confidence to navigate these situations when they occur. Encourage your child to set social goals, like introducing themselves to two new people or participating in a group game. These goals provide a sense of purpose and achievement.

It's also wise to have a backup plan. Bring something small that your child enjoys, like playing cards or memory cards, but try to avoid tablets and phones. These items can serve as a calming distraction if your child starts to feel overwhelmed but won't isolate them from the social environment. Tablets and phones tend to cause ADHD children to enter into their hyper focused state and completely withdraw from social gatherings.

Managing social interactions at gatherings requires practical strategies. Teach your child simple introduction phrases like, "Hi, I'm [Name]. What's your name?" This breaks the ice and makes it easier for them to engage with others. Emphasize the importance of kindness and manners. Explain that small acts of kindness and good manners can make a big difference in how others perceive and treat them. Encourage your child to join group activities. Let them observe for a bit if they're shy, and then gently encourage them to participate. This gradual approach can make them feel more comfortable. Prepare them for handling rejection. Explain that not everyone will want to play or talk with them, and that's okay. Teach them to find another activity or group to join.

As a parent, your support during the event is invaluable. Stay nearby to offer a sense of security without hovering. Periodically check in with your child to see how they're doing. A quick thumbs-up or a brief conversation is effective. Providing breaks is essential. Allow your child to take a moment to regroup if needed. Offering a healthy snack can serve as a natural break, giving them time to recharge without feeling like they're missing out.

Debriefing after the event is just as important as the preparation. Take the time to talk with your child about their experiences. Ask open-ended questions like, "How did you feel about the event?" or "What did you expect going in?" These questions encourage your child to reflect on their experiences and express their feelings. Highlight the positive moments, focusing on what went well. Build their confidence and reinforce their social skills with this tactic. If there were any challenges, discuss them calmly and constructively. Offer solutions and strategies for handling similar situations in the future.

By taking these steps, you help your child navigate social gatherings with greater confidence and ease. Preparing them for what to expect, providing strategies for managing interactions, and offering your support throughout the event can significantly improve their ability to enjoy and benefit from social situations. Debriefing afterward ensures they learn from each experience, building the skills and confidence they need to thrive in social settings.

Navigating social gatherings and events can be complex, but with preparation, support, and reflection, your child can learn to handle these situations more confidently. The skills they learn will make social interactions more enjoyable and contribute to their overall development and well-being.

SELF-CARE FOR PARENTS

Parenting a child with ADHD often feels like running a never-ending marathon. You wake up each day ready to tackle the challenges, only to find yourself exhausted before the day is halfway through. You juggle appointments, school meetings, and endless energy bursts, all while trying to maintain your sanity. The relentless pace can take a toll, making self-care not just a luxury but a necessity. Recognizing and managing your stress is crucial to being the supportive, patient parent your child needs.

STRESS MANAGEMENT TECHNIQUES FOR PARENTS

Recognizing the signs of stress is the first step toward managing it effectively. Stress can manifest in various ways, and it's essential to identify these early signs before they escalate into burnout. Physical symptoms such as headaches, fatigue, and muscle tension are common indicators that your body is under strain. You might find yourself dealing with persistent headaches that no amount of over-the-counter medication can alleviate. Fatigue becomes a constant companion, making it hard to get through the day. Muscle tension, especially in the neck and shoulders, is another telltale sign that stress is taking its toll on your body.

Emotional symptoms are equally important to recognize. Irritability, anxiety, and depression can creep in, often unnoticed, until they start affecting your daily interactions and overall well-being. You may find yourself snapping at your child or partner over minor issues, feeling anxious about things that never used to bother you, or sinking into a sadness that seems to have no apparent cause. Behavioral changes such as alterations in eating or sleeping patterns are also red flags. You may start eating more or less than usual, seeking comfort in food, or losing your appetite altogether. Sleep disturbances, whether it's trouble falling asleep, staying asleep, or waking up feeling unrested, are common among stressed parents.

Practicing mindfulness and relaxation techniques can provide immediate relief from stress. Mindful breathing, for instance, involves focusing on your breath to center your mind. A specific technique known as box breathing, which involves inhaling for four counts, holding the breath for four counts, exhaling for four counts, and holding again for four counts, has been shown to lower heart rate and blood pressure by 10 percent in less than five minutes. Progressive muscle relaxation is another effective method. This technique involves tensing and relaxing each muscle group, starting from your toes and working your way up to your head. Guided imagery, where you visualize calming scenes or places, can also transport your mind to a peaceful state, reducing stress and promoting relaxation.

Engaging in regular physical activity is a powerful antidote to stress. Exercise releases endorphins, the body's natural feel-good chemicals, which can elevate your mood and improve your overall sense of well-being. For parents with ADHD, physical activity is doubly beneficial. It helps manage your symptoms, providing an outlet for the energy bursts and restlessness you might experience. Aerobic exercises like walking, jogging, swimming, and playing sports like pickleball or basketball are excellent for getting your heart rate up and releasing built-up tension. Strength training, whether through weightlifting or resistance bands, builds muscle strength and resilience, giving you a physical and mental boost. Mind-body exercises like yoga and Pilates offer the added benefits of improving flexibility, balance, and mindfulness, helping you stay grounded and centered.

A daily self-care routine can provide a structured way to incorporate relaxation, physical health, and mental health care into your life. Start your day with morning rituals such as stretching, meditation, or journaling. Stretching helps wake up your body and release any tension that may have built up overnight. Meditation, even for a few minutes, can set a calm and focused tone for the day. Journaling allows you to process your thoughts and emotions, providing clarity and a sense of release. Midday breaks are essential for maintaining your energy levels and focus. Short walks around the block, deep breathing exercises, or even a quick stretch at your desk can refresh your mind and body, preventing the buildup of stress.

In the evening, unwind with activities that promote relaxation and prepare you for a restful night's sleep. Reading a book, taking a warm bath, or listening to soothing music or audiobooks can help transition your mind and body from the busyness of the day to a calm state.

Interactive Element: Daily Self-Care Routine Planner

Creating a self-care routine can be daunting, but breaking it into manageable parts makes it easier to stick to. Use the following planner to structure your day:

1. **Morning Rituals**:

- **Stretching**: 5–10 minutes of gentle stretching.
- **Meditation**: 5 minutes of mindful breathing or guided meditation.
- **Journaling**: Write down three things you're grateful for or thoughts you need to process.

2. **Midday Breaks**:

- **Short Walks**: 10–15 minutes around your neighborhood or workplace.
- **Deep Breathing**: 5 minutes of box breathing or another breathing technique.
- **Quick Stretching**: 5 minutes focusing on areas where you feel tension.

3. **Evening Unwind**:

- **Reading**: Spend 15–30 minutes reading a good book.
- **Warm Bath**: Take a warm bath with calming scents.
- **Listening to Music or Audiobooks**: Choose something soothing and enjoyable.

Integrating these practices into your daily routine allows you to manage stress more effectively and maintain balance and well-being.

BUILDING YOUR SUPPORT NETWORK

Building a robust support network is one of the most powerful steps you can take as a parent of a neurodivergent child. The journey can be overwhelming, but you don't have to walk it alone. Your support network can include family members, friends, and community resources, all of whom can provide emotional support, practical advice, and a sense of community.

First, look to your family. Siblings, parents, and extended family members can be invaluable sources of support. They often deeply understand your family's dynamics and can offer practical and heartfelt help. Perhaps your sibling can take your child for an afternoon, giving you a much-needed break. Or maybe your parents can provide wisdom and comfort based on their experiences. Feel free to reach out to these close connections; they often want to help but may only know how if you ask.

Friends also play a crucial role in your support network. Close friends, especially those who are parents themselves, can offer empathy and practical advice. Parent groups provide a space to share experiences, ask questions, and receive support, whether formal or informal. These groups can be a lifeline, offering a sense of camaraderie and understanding that is hard to find elsewhere. When your child is having a particularly tough day, a quick chat with a friend who gets it can make all the difference.

Community resources are another essential part of your support network. Local support groups for parents of children with ADHD, community centers that offer relevant programs, and even your child's teachers can be valuable allies. These resources can provide practical advice, educational workshops, and emotional support. Check your community center's bulletin board or website for information on support groups and workshops.

Don't overlook your child's school; teachers and school counselors can offer insights and support tailored to your child's educational environment.

Joining or forming support groups can provide additional layers of support. Local support groups often have regular meeting schedules and may require a small joining fee. These groups offer a structured environment where you can share experiences and strategies with other parents who understand your challenges. If you can't find a local group, consider online communities. Forums and social media groups can be incredibly supportive, offering 24/7 access to advice and camaraderie. If there are no existing groups that meet your needs, consider starting your own. Find members through community bulletin boards or online platforms and set meeting agendas that address common concerns and strategies.

Professional support is another important component. Seeking professional help, such as counseling or coaching, can provide targeted strategies and emotional support. It's often best to avoid psychiatrists at first, as they may be quick to prescribe medication. ADHD coaches, who specialize in helping both parents and kids manage ADHD, can offer practical strategies tailored to your specific situation. Medical professionals like pediatricians and psychologists can comprehensively assess your child's needs and help you develop a holistic management plan.

Fostering reciprocal support relationships can create a sense of community and shared responsibility. Babysitting swaps with other parents allow you to take breaks while knowing your child is in capable hands. Organizing group outings or playdates, such as barbecues or trips to the park, can provide socialization opportunities for your child and support for you. Include the whole family whenever possible, as this fosters a sense of community and shared experiences. Emotional support is equally important. Regular check-ins and conversations with a trusted friend or family member can provide a safe space to vent and discuss your feelings. Sometimes, simply talking about your challenges can be incredibly therapeutic.

Visual Element: Support Network Worksheet

Creating a support network worksheet or mapping this out in your head can help you identify and organize your sources of support. Use the following template to get started:

Family Support:

1. **Siblings**:

- Name:
- Contact Information:
- Type of Support:

2. **Parents**:

- Name:
- Contact Information:
- Type of Support:

3. **Extended Family**:

- Name:
- Contact Information:
- Type of Support:

Friends:

1. Close Friends:

- Name:
- Contact Information:
- Type of Support:

2. Parent Groups:

- Name:
- Contact Information:
- Meeting Schedule:

Community Resources:

1. Local Support Groups:

- Name:
- Contact Information:
- Meeting Schedule:

2. Community Centers:

- Name:
- Contact Information:
- Available Programs:

3. Teachers:

- Name:
- Contact Information:
- Type of Support:

Professional Support:

1. **Therapists**:

   - Name:
   - Contact Information:
   - Type of Support:

2. **ADHD Coaches**:

   - Name:
   - Contact Information:
   - Type of Support:

3. **Medical Professionals**:

   - Name:
   - Contact Information:
   - Type of Support:

Reciprocal Support Relationships:

1. **Babysitting Swaps**:

   - Name:
   - Contact Information:
   - Schedule:

2. **Shared Activities**:

   - Type:
   - Participants:
   - Schedule:

3. **Emotional Support**:

- Name:
- Contact Information:
- Type of Support:

Fill out this worksheet to visualize your support network and identify any gaps. This exercise can help you see where you may need to reach out for additional support or where you can offer support to others.

FINDING TIME FOR SELF-CARE AMID THE CHAOS

As a parent of a neurodivergent child, the whirlwind of daily responsibilities can make self-care seem like an unattainable luxury. However, prioritizing self-care is not just beneficial—it's necessary. Viewing self-care as essential rather than optional can be a significant mindset shift. This change in perspective helps you recognize that taking care of yourself enables you to be more patient, present, and effective in caring for your child. To prioritize self-care, start by blocking time in your calendar specifically for these activities. Treat these appointments with yourself as non-negotiable, just like any other important meeting. Identifying what activities rejuvenate you and what inspires negative emotions is also crucial. Perhaps you find solace in reading a book or walking in nature, whereas watching the news on TV news leaves you feeling negative emotions or more stressed. Avoid activities that drain you and focus on those that replenish your energy.

Creating a flexible self-care plan tailored to your changing schedule and needs can help ensure that self-care remains a consistent part of your life. Daily self-care activities can be short and easily integrated into your routine. For instance, you might spend ten minutes in the morning sipping a cup of tea while listening to your favorite music. Weekly indulgences, like a more extended bath, a visit to a yoga class, or a round of golf or pickleball, can provide more profound relaxation and rejuvenation. It's also beneficial to have emergency self-care strategies for high-stress moments. These quick fixes include a five-minute breathing exercise or a brief walk around the block to reset your mind and body.

Finding and using small pockets of time throughout the day for self-care can make a significant difference. Micro-meditations—short, mindful breathing sessions—can be done in just a few minutes but offer substantial stress relief. Expressing gratitude by jotting down daily positives in a journal can shift your focus toward what's going well, providing a mental boost. Quick exercises like stretching, short walks, or desk workouts can fit even the busiest schedules. These small but consistent actions can accumulate, leading to a noticeable improvement in your overall well-being.

Delegating and sharing responsibilities within the household is another fundamental strategy for freeing up time for self-care. Distributing household chores among family members lightens your load and fosters a sense of shared responsibility and teamwork. Consider outsourcing tasks like cleaning or running errands if they fit within your budget. Hiring help, even for just a few hours a week, can provide you with much-needed time to focus on yourself. Partner support is equally important. Sharing parenting tasks with your partner ensures you have time to rest and recharge, preventing burnout and promoting a balanced partnership.

By prioritizing self-care, creating a flexible plan, using small pockets of time, and delegating responsibilities, you can maintain your well-being amid the chaos of parenting. Self-care is not a luxury; it's a necessity that enables you to be the best parent you can be for your ADHD child. Taking care of yourself is the foundation for taking care of your family.

BUILDING A SUPPORTIVE COMMUNITY

Imagine standing in a crowded room, feeling like everyone speaks a different language. No one seems to understand the unique challenges you face daily. As a parent of a child with ADHD, this feeling of isolation can be overwhelming. However, finding a supportive community can transform this experience, turning isolation into connection and confusion into clarity. Building a supportive community is not just beneficial; it's essential. It offers emotional support, practical advice, and a sense of belonging that can make a world of difference in your journey.

JOINING LOCAL AND ONLINE SUPPORT GROUPS

Support groups provide a sanctuary where you can share experiences, gain practical advice, and feel understood. They offer a space to speak openly about your challenges without fear of judgment. When you connect with other parents who face similar struggles, you find emotional support that is comforting and empowering. Sharing experiences and feelings in these groups can be a cathartic release, allowing you to vent frustrations and celebrate victories with those who truly understand. Hearing others' stories can also offer new perspectives and strategies, enriching your approach to parenting.

Practical advice is another invaluable benefit of support groups. Parents who have navigated similar paths can share what has worked for them, providing you with a treasure trove of strategies and tips. Whether it's managing meltdowns, handling homework, or finding suitable therapies, collective wisdom can offer solutions you may not have considered. Learning from others' experiences can save you time and effort, helping you avoid common pitfalls and implement effective strategies more quickly.

The most profound benefit of joining a support group is feeling understood and not alone. The sense of community that develops in these groups can be a lifeline, offering a sense of belonging and camaraderie. Knowing that others face the same challenges can be incredibly reassuring, reducing feelings of isolation and boosting your resilience. In a support group, you are part of a tribe that shares your journey, offering mutual support and understanding.

Finding local support groups can be a rewarding endeavor. Start by checking community centers and local community boards, which often list support groups and other resources for parents. Medical offices can also be valuable; ask your child's pediatrician or therapist for recommendations. Schools are another great place to inquire about parent groups explicitly organized for parents of children with ADHD. These groups can offer a wealth of information and support, often led by experienced facilitators who can guide discussions and provide valuable insights.

Online support groups offer unique advantages, especially for busy parents who may find it challenging to attend in-person meetings. Social media platforms like Facebook host numerous groups dedicated to parents of children with ADHD. These groups allow real-time interactions, enabling you to seek advice and support whenever needed. Specialized forums like ADDitude and CHADD online groups provide a wealth of information and a supportive community of parents and experts. Virtual support group sessions, often held via Zoom or other online meeting platforms, offer the benefits of face-to-face interaction without the need to leave your home.

Participating effectively in support groups involves more than just attending meetings or reading posts. Being open and honest about your experiences can foster deeper connections and provide more meaningful support. Sharing your successes and struggles helps others feel less alone and encourages them to share their stories. Asking questions is another important aspect of effective participation. Seeking advice and recommendations from others can provide new strategies and insights you may not have considered. Offering support to others in the group is equally important. Giving encouragement and sharing what has worked for you can help others navigate their challenges. Respecting confidentiality within the group is crucial for maintaining trust and creating a safe space where everyone feels comfortable sharing.

Support Group Engagement Tips

1. **Be Open and Honest**: Share your experiences, both successes and struggles, to foster deeper connections.
2. **Ask Questions**: Seek advice and recommendations to gain new strategies and insights.
3. **Offer Support**: Provide encouragement and share what has worked for you to help others navigate their challenges.

4. **Respect Confidentiality**: Maintain privacy and trust within the group to create a safe and supportive environment.

By actively engaging in local and online support groups, you can build a supportive community offering emotional support, practical advice, and a sense of belonging. This community can be a lifeline, providing the understanding and resources you need to navigate the challenges of parenting. Whether through in-person meetings or online interactions, the connections you make in these groups can offer invaluable support and guidance, helping you feel less isolated and more empowered on your journey.

ENGAGING WITH COMMUNITY RESOURCES

Navigating the world of community resources can feel overwhelming, but these resources can provide invaluable support for families of neurodivergent children. Community resources come in many forms, from educational workshops and recreational programs to health services. Each resource type offers unique benefits to help you and your child thrive.

Educational resources are a cornerstone of community support. Workshops, seminars, and classes designed for parents and children dealing with ADHD can provide practical knowledge and skills. These events often feature experts who share the latest research and strategies for managing ADHD. They can cover various topics, from behavioral interventions to academic accommodations. Attending these events can equip you with the tools to support your child more effectively.

Recreational programs offer another layer of support by providing structured activities that can help your child develop social skills, build self-esteem, and burn off excess energy. Sports teams, for example, provide physical exercise and teach teamwork, discipline, and social interaction. Local leagues are a great place to start, offering various sports catering to different interests and abilities. Art classes provide a creative outlet, allowing them to express themselves and improve their focus through structured yet flexible activities. Community centers often host organized events and activities that are both fun and educational, providing a safe space for your child to engage with peers. Specialized summer camps for ADHD children can offer tailored programs that address your child's unique needs, providing fun and therapeutic benefits.

Health services are another important community resource. Speech therapy, occupational therapy, and behavioral therapy are commonly recommended to help children with ADHD develop essential skills. Speech therapy can improve communication skills, occupational therapy can enhance fine motor skills and daily living activities, and behavioral therapy can provide strategies for managing challenging behaviors. Supportive counseling, whether individual or family therapy, can help you and your child navigate the emotional complexities of ADHD. Family therapy sessions can be particularly beneficial in fostering understanding and cooperation among family members, creating a more harmonious home environment.

Accessing these educational resources involves a bit of legwork but is well worth the effort. Start by attending ADHD-focused workshops and seminars. These events are often advertised through community centers, local clinics, and schools. They provide a wealth of information and the opportunity to network with other parents and professionals. Don't overlook your local library, which can be a treasure trove of resources. Libraries often have books, DVDs, and online materials specifically about ADHD, offering a convenient and cost-effective way to educate yourself. Consulting with local experts, such as school counselors or educational psychologists, can provide valuable insights and recommendations tailored to your child's needs.

Participating in recreational programs requires finding activities that align with your child's interests and needs. Look into local leagues for sports teams that offer structure and social interaction. Many communities have recreational centers that provide a range of sports, from soccer to swimming, catering to various skill levels. You can find art classes at community centers, art studios, or through local educational institutions. These classes provide a structured environment where your child can explore their creativity while improving focus and self-discipline. Community centers often host events and activities that are both engaging and educational, providing a social outlet in a safe and supervised setting. Specialized summer camps designed for children with ADHD offer tailored programs that address your child's therapeutic and recreational needs, providing a supportive environment where they can thrive.

Using health services involves finding the right professionals to provide the support and interventions your child needs. Start by looking for local clinics that specialize in ADHD. These clinics often have a team of specialists, including pediatricians, psychologists, and therapists, who can provide comprehensive care. Access therapy services like speech, occupational, and behavioral therapy through local hospitals, private practices, or community health centers. These therapies offer targeted interventions to address your child's specific challenges. Supportive counseling, whether through individual therapy or family sessions, can provide emotional support and practical strategies for managing ADHD. Family therapy can be particularly beneficial in fostering understanding and cooperation among family members, helping to create a more supportive and harmonious home environment.

By engaging with these community resources, you can build a robust support network that provides practical help, emotional support, and valuable knowledge. Whether it's attending workshops, enrolling in recreational programs, or accessing health services, these resources can make a significant difference in your family's journey with ADHD. The key is to explore the options available in your community, take advantage of the resources that resonate with your needs, and actively participate in the opportunities they offer.

CREATING A SUPPORTIVE FAMILY NETWORK

Building a supportive family network is crucial for managing ADHD and ensuring a cohesive, nurturing environment. The foundation of this network lies in emotional support, shared responsibilities, and consistent strategies. A strong family network provides a solid emotional foundation, helping each member feel understood and valued. When everyone in the household is on the same page, it creates a sense of unity and stability. This unity is particularly important for children with ADHD, who thrive in environments where they feel safe and supported.

Shared responsibilities are another critical component of a supportive family network. Distributing tasks and roles among family members ensures that no one person bears the entire burden. This approach not only alleviates stress for the primary caregiver but also fosters a sense of teamwork and cooperation. Assigning specific tasks to each family member, whether helping with homework, managing appointments, or preparing meals, can make daily life more manageable. It also teaches children valuable life skills and promotes a sense of responsibility.

Consistency is vital when it comes to managing ADHD. A unified approach to strategies and interventions ensures everyone is working toward the same goals. Consistent routines, rules, and expectations help children understand what is expected of them, reducing anxiety and improving behavior. When all family members use the same techniques and language, it creates a seamless and supportive environment that reinforces positive behavior.

Effective communication within the family is essential for maintaining a supportive network. Regular family meetings provide an opportunity to discuss concerns, share updates, and plan for the future. These meetings create a space where everyone can voice their opinions and contribute to decision-making. Defining clear roles for each family member helps ensure that responsibilities are understood and tasks are completed. Encouraging open dialogue allows for questions and feedback, fostering a sense of inclusion and collaboration.

Educating the extended family about ADHD is also important for building a supportive network. Grandparents, aunts, uncles, and other relatives play a significant role in a child's life. Providing them with accurate information and resources can help dispel myths and misconceptions. Open discussions about the child's specific needs and challenges can foster understanding and empathy. Involving extended family in routines and demonstrating strategies and techniques can help them feel more confident and capable of providing support.

Family bonding activities are a fantastic way to promote teamwork and ensure everyone feels included and supported. Family game nights offer a fun and engaging way to spend time together, fostering communication and cooperation. Choose games everyone can enjoy and participate in, ensuring that the focus is on fun and connection rather than competition. Outdoor activities like hiking, biking, or picnics provide an opportunity to enjoy nature and engage in physical exercise, which benefits everyone, especially children with ADHD. Collaborative projects like working on a family art project or garden encourage creativity and teamwork. These activities allow family members to work toward a common goal, strengthening bonds, creating lasting memories, and celebrating successes together, whether big or small, reinforcing positive behavior and promoting a sense of achievement and pride.

Building a supportive family network is a cornerstone of managing ADHD effectively. Emotional support, shared responsibilities, and consistent strategies create a nurturing environment where your child can thrive. Open communication and educating extended family members foster understanding and empathy, while family bonding activities promote teamwork and connection. The next chapter will explore long-term strategies for success, ensuring that the progress you make continues to benefit your child in the years to come.

LONG-TERM STRATEGIES FOR SUCCESS

Imagine your child standing at the edge of a diving board, ready to leap into the deep end of adolescence. The water below represents a mix of new challenges and opportunities, some visible and some lurking beneath the surface. As your child transitions into adolescence, the waters become more profound and complex, requiring new skills and strategies to navigate successfully. This chapter aims to equip you with the tools and insights needed to support your child through this significant phase of growth and development.

TRANSITIONING TO ADOLESCENCE: NEW CHALLENGES AND SOLUTIONS

Adolescence is a time of immense change, and for children with ADHD, these changes can present unique challenges. The increased academic demands, complex social dynamics, and hormonal fluctuations can amplify the difficulties they already face. Understanding these challenges is the first step in helping your child navigate this turbulent period.

Academic challenges often intensify during adolescence—the expectations and workload increase, requiring more advanced organizational and time management skills. Your child may need help keeping track of assignments, managing long-term projects, and balancing multiple subjects. To support them, consider introducing planners and apps specifically designed for scheduling. These tools can help your child break down tasks into manageable steps, set reminders, and allocate specific times for each subject. Encouraging the development of effective study habits and techniques is also crucial. For example, teaching your child to use the Pomodoro Technique—working in focused intervals with short breaks—can improve their productivity and reduce feeling overwhelmed.

Social dynamics become more intricate during adolescence as peer relationships are more significant. Navigating these relationships can be particularly challenging for children with ADHD, who may struggle with impulsivity and social cues. Enhancing their communication and conflict-resolution skills can make a significant difference. Role-playing different social scenarios can help your child practice these skills in a safe environment. Encourage them to join clubs or groups that align with their interests, providing opportunities to make friends in structured settings where they feel confident.

Emotional fluctuations are a hallmark of adolescence, with mood swings and stress becoming more pronounced due to hormonal changes. Teaching your child self-awareness and self-management skills can help them take more responsibility for their ADHD. Journals or apps designed for self-monitoring can be valuable tools. Encourage your child to track their behaviors, moods, and triggers, helping them identify patterns and develop strategies for managing their emotions. Establishing personal and academic goals can also provide direction and motivation.

Encourage your child to reflect regularly on their progress, celebrate their achievements, and address any setbacks constructively.

Providing emotional and mental health support is essential during adolescence. Whether through school or privately, counseling services can offer a safe space for your child to explore their feelings and develop coping strategies. Peer support groups specifically for teens with ADHD can provide a sense of community and understanding. These groups offer a platform for sharing experiences, learning from peers, and building resilience. Encourage your child to engage in stress-relief activities that they enjoy, such as hobbies, sports, or creative pursuits. These activities can provide a healthy outlet for their energy and emotions, promoting overall well-being.

Interactive Element: Self-Monitoring Journal Template

Daily Log:

- **Mood:** Happy, sad, angry, anxious, excited
- **Energy Level:** Low, moderate, high
- **Tasks Completed:** Homework, chores, extracurricular activities
- **Triggers Noted:** Stressors or events that impacted mood or behavior
- **Reflection:** Thoughts on what went well and areas for improvement

This self-monitoring journal template allows your child to develop greater self-awareness and learn to manage their ADHD more effectively. Encourage them to review their entries regularly, identify patterns, and discuss strategies for improvement.

As your child navigates adolescence, the support and strategies you provide can significantly affect their ability to manage ADHD and thrive. Addressing academic challenges, enhancing social skills, promoting self-awareness, and providing emotional support can help your child build the resilience and skills they need for long-term success.

PREPARING FOR INDEPENDENCE: LIFE SKILLS FOR ADHD TEENS

As your child moves toward independence, it becomes imperative to teach essential life skills. These skills lay the foundation for self-sufficiency and help teens navigate daily challenges. Start with household chores. Cooking, cleaning, and laundry may seem basic, but they are vital for independent living. Begin with simple recipes, gradually introducing more complex dishes. Use visual aids like recipe cards with step-by-step instructions. Cleaning tasks can be broken down into manageable parts, like setting a timer for fifteen-minute cleaning sprints. Laundry can be taught with a checklist detailing each step, from sorting clothes to folding them.

Financial literacy is another critical area. Teach your teen the basics of budgeting, saving, and spending responsibly. Start with a simple budget template where they can track their income and expenses. Discuss the concept of saving for larger goals, like a new gadget or a trip. Use real-life scenarios, such as comparing prices at the grocery store, to teach intelligent spending habits. Encourage them to open a savings account and set financial goals, fostering a sense of responsibility and planning for the future.

Time management is a skill that can significantly improve your teen's ability to handle responsibilities. Introduce them to planners and scheduling apps. Help them prioritize tasks by importance and deadline. Teach them to allocate specific times for each activity, ensuring they balance schoolwork, chores, and leisure. Highlight the importance of setting reminders and alarms to stay on track. These tools can help them develop a routine and reduce the overwhelm often accompanying ADHD.

Academic and career planning skills are also vital. Start by exploring your teen's interests. Identify their strengths and passions, encouraging them to pursue activities aligned with these areas. Set short-term and long-term academic goals, breaking them down into achievable steps. Career exploration can begin with job shadowing or internships, providing real-world experience. Career counseling can offer further guidance, helping them understand the educational paths required for their chosen careers. Encourage them to seek opportunities that align with their interests, fostering a sense of purpose and direction.

Decision-making and problem-solving abilities are essential for adulthood. Introduce decision-making frameworks like pros and cons lists, helping your teen weigh options and make informed choices. Teach problem-solving steps such as identifying the problem, brainstorming potential solutions, and evaluating the outcomes. Real-life practice can be invaluable. Involve your teen in family decision-making processes, giving them a voice in discussions and helping them understand the impact of their choices. This involvement builds confidence and hones their decision-making skills.

Encouraging self-advocacy and communication is equally important. Self-advocacy training can involve practicing speaking up for their needs in different scenarios, from school settings to social interactions. Strong verbal and written communication skills can empower them to express themselves clearly and confidently. Role-playing real-life conversations can provide practice in a safe environment, building their confidence for actual interactions. Emphasize the importance of clear and respectful communication, teaching them to articulate their thoughts and needs effectively.

These life skills are invaluable as your teen prepares for independence. They provide the tools needed to navigate adulthood with confidence and competence. Teaching these skills requires patience and consistency, but the rewards are significant. Your teen will not only gain independence but also build a strong foundation for a successful and fulfilling life.

MAINTAINING PROGRESS: CONSISTENCY AND ADAPTATION

Maintaining consistent routines is crucial for the continued success of children with ADHD, even as they grow older. A daily schedule serves as a framework that provides stability and predictability. A consistent routine helps reduce anxiety and confusion, making it easier to focus on the tasks at hand. Establishing clear rules and consequences creates an environment where expectations are understood. This clarity is essential for maintaining good behavior and academic progress. Regular check-ins and adjustments to these routines ensure that they remain effective and relevant as your child grows. Monitoring progress through these check-ins allows you to see what's working and what may need tweaking.

As children grow, their needs and challenges change. The strategies that worked when they were younger may require adjustments to remain effective. Regularly assessing the effectiveness of current methods is critical. This evaluation helps you identify areas that need improvement. A particular approach to homework is no longer practical, or new social dynamics at school require different support strategies. Tweaking routines and interventions as needed ensures your child receives the appropriate support. Involving your child in the adaptation process can be incredibly beneficial. Seeking their feedback helps you understand their perspective and makes them feel valued. It also encourages them to take ownership of their routines and strategies, fostering a sense of responsibility.

Encouraging self-monitoring and reflection can further enhance your child's ability to manage their ADHD. Keeping a daily or weekly journal can be a powerful tool for self-awareness. Your child can track their moods, behaviors, and triggers through journaling. This self-assessment helps them recognize patterns and understand the impact of their actions. Using checklists or rating scales can provide a structured way for them to evaluate their progress. Reflective conversations between you and your child about their journal entries can open up valuable discussions. These regular discussions about progress and areas for improvement reinforce the habit of self-reflection and self-monitoring.

Empowering your child to set goals and track progress fosters a sense of ownership and accountability. Collaborative goal-setting involves working together to identify realistic and meaningful goals. This collaboration ensures the goals align with your child's interests and capabilities. Tracking progress through charts, apps, or journals helps your child see their achievements and understand what it takes to reach their goals. Celebrating these milestones, no matter how small, provides positive reinforcement and motivation. Recognizing and rewarding achievements helps build your child's confidence and encourages continued effort.

Interactive Element: Goal-Setting Worksheet

- **Goal:** Clearly define the goal (e.g., "Complete homework before dinner each night").

- **Steps to Achieve Goal:** Break down the goal into smaller, manageable steps (e.g., "1. Gather supplies, 2. Set a timer for 20 minutes, 3. Take a 5-minute break").
- **Track Progress:** Use a chart or app to mark each step completed.
- **Reflection:** Regularly review progress and discuss what's working and what needs adjustment.
- **Rewards:** Identify rewards for achieving milestones (e.g., extra leisure time, a special treat).

By using this goal-setting worksheet, you and your child can work together to set and achieve meaningful goals. This collaborative approach helps your child stay on track and fosters a sense of accomplishment and self-discipline.

Progress in managing ADHD is an ongoing process that requires consistency, adaptation, self-monitoring, and collaborative goal-setting. By implementing these strategies, you can help your child navigate the challenges of ADHD and build a foundation for long-term success.

CELEBRATING MILESTONES: RECOGNIZING ACHIEVEMENTS ALONG THE WAY

Recognizing and celebrating milestones is pivotal for building self-esteem and motivation in children with ADHD. Celebrations serve as positive reinforcement, which can significantly boost confidence and morale. When you acknowledge your child's achievements, no matter how small, you send a powerful message: their efforts are valued, and their hard work pays off. This recognition encourages them to keep trying, even when tasks seem daunting. It also creates positive memories that you both can look back on with pride. Celebrating successes together strengthens your bond and provides a joyful counterbalance to the struggles that often come with ADHD.

Identifying milestones to celebrate is the next step. Academic achievements are obvious choices, such as improved grades, completed projects, or consistent homework completion. But pay attention to behavioral improvements. If your child has consistently followed routines or shown better self-control, these milestones are worth celebrating. Personal growth is equally important. Has your child developed a new skill or hobby? Have they improved social interactions or taken on new responsibilities at home? These are all milestones that reflect their growth and resilience. By identifying and celebrating various achievements, you help your child see their progress in multiple areas of their life.

Creative ways to celebrate these milestones can make the recognition even more meaningful. Family celebrations, such as special dinners, outings, or small parties, can provide a sense of occasion and importance. Personal rewards, like small gifts or privileges, can be tailored to your child's interests and serve as tangible reminders of their achievements. Public recognition can also be potent. Sharing your child's successes with extended family or friends can provide an additional layer of encouragement and pride. Whether it's a phone call to grandparents or a shout-out on social media, public recognition can amplify the positive impact of the celebration.

Fostering a culture of celebration within your family can make these moments a regular and expected part of life. Monthly check-ins where you review and celebrate progress can help keep the focus on growth and improvement. An achievement board displayed in a common area of your home can visually showcase your child's accomplishments, constantly reminding them of their successes. Encouraging daily gratitude practices can also contribute to this positive culture. By regularly acknowledging and appreciating the good things in life, you help your child develop a mindset that looks for and values progress and effort.

Creating a family culture that regularly acknowledges and celebrates achievements fosters an environment of positivity and encouragement. This not only boosts your child's morale but also strengthens family bonds. When celebrations become a regular part of your routine, they reinforce the idea that effort and progress are always worth recognizing. This culture of celebration can provide the emotional support and motivation your child needs to navigate the challenges of ADHD, turning each milestone into a stepping stone toward greater confidence and success.

A CHANCE TO HELP OTHER FAMILIES

There's no denying that parenting a child with ADHD comes with its challenges, but when you know more about how to help them, it's very rewarding too. Why not take a moment now to help other parents find those rewards?

Simply by sharing your honest opinion of this book and a little about how it's helped you, you'll make it easier for other parents to find it and pick up the strategies they need to help their own super-kids.

WANT TO HELP OTHERS?

Thank you so much for your support. I wish you and your family all the best going forward.

Scan the QR code below

CONCLUSION

Reflecting on our journey together shows that we've explored the vast landscape of parenting a child with ADHD. My mission has been to provide you with both practical strategies and emotional support, helping you navigate the unique challenges and celebrate the extraordinary strengths of your super-kid. This journey has not only been about managing ADHD symptoms but also about fostering a nurturing and stable family environment that allows everyone to thrive.

Chapter 2 delved into the importance of building effective routines and structures. We discussed how morning, homework, and bedtime routines can transform chaotic days into well-organized and predictable ones. Implementing visual aids, checklists, and timers can help your child stay focused and feel more in control. These small changes can significantly improve daily life, reducing anxiety for you and your child.

Chapter 4 focused on emotional regulation and self-control. We explored mindfulness practices and breathing techniques to help your child navigate their emotions. By teaching your child to recognize and express their feelings, you equip them with essential tools for emotional balance. These skills not only help manage ADHD symptoms but also contribute to their overall well-being and resilience.

In Chapter 5, we looked at positive reinforcement and behavior management. We emphasized the importance of using positive reinforcement to encourage desired behaviors. Creating effective behavior charts and offering meaningful rewards can motivate your child to stay on track. We also discussed why medication should be considered a last resort while exploring natural supplements and holistic approaches should be the first. These strategies help build a supportive environment that fosters growth and self-regulation.

Chapter 7 was all about collaborating with educators and schools. We discussed the significance of advocating for Individualized Education Programs (IEPs) and 504 Plans to ensure your child receives the support they need. Building strong relationships with teachers and maintaining open communication is crucial for your child's academic success. By working together with educators, you create a team dedicated to helping your child thrive.

In Chapter 10, we celebrated the unique strengths of children with ADHD. We explored how discovering and nurturing these strengths can empower your child. Real-life success stories illustrated the potential for extraordinary achievements. Encouraging your child to set goals and providing opportunities for success can boost their confidence and self-esteem. Recognizing and celebrating their talents helps them see ADHD not as a hindrance but as a unique aspect of who they are.

Chapter 12 focused on you, the parent. We acknowledged the importance of self-care and stress management. Parenting a neurodivergent child is demanding, and taking care of yourself is essential. Building a support network, engaging in regular physical activity, and practicing mindfulness can help you stay resilient. By prioritizing your well-being, you set a positive example for your child and create a stable foundation for your family's happiness.

Key takeaways from our journey include the understanding that ADHD does not have to be a hinderance but with some tailored tactics for your super-kid, a unique superpower for your child. Medication should be the last resort, with natural supplements and holistic approaches considered first. Positive reinforcement should always exceed punishment to encourage desired behaviors. Use the resources around you, from support groups to educational tools. Be a team for your kids, working with educators and family members. Implement consistent systems and routines to provide stability and predictability.

As you continue to implement these strategies in your child's life, consider adopting a couple for yourself. Whether practicing mindfulness, setting personal goals, or building a support network, you'll quickly see the difference in your well-being. Caring for yourself provides an excellent example for your child to emulate.

Remember, you're not alone on this journey. Many parents share similar challenges and triumphs. Your dedication and efforts will lead to a more stable, loving, and thriving family life. Celebrate the small victories, stay resilient during tough times, and always cherish the unique strengths your child brings to your family. You are doing an incredible job; your love and support make all the difference. Together, you and your super-kid can navigate the world with confidence and joy.

REFERENCES

Abbey Clinic. "The Role of a Consistent ADHD Schedule." *Abbey Neuropsychology Clinic* (blog), January 16, 2024. https://www.abbeyneuropsychologyclinic.com/the-role-of-a-consistent-adhd-schedule/.

"ADHD and School (for Parents)." https://kidshealth.org/en/parents/adhd-school.html.

"ADHD Entrepreneur Stories: JetBlue, Kinko's, Jupitermedia." https://www.additudemag.com/adhd-entrepreneur-stories-jetblue-kinkos-jupitermedia/.

"ADHD Homework Strategies: Study Smarter, Not Harder!" https://www.additudemag.com/slideshows/adhd-homework-strategies-and-shortcuts/.

ADHD, Next Step 4. "Parenting a Child with ADHD: 5 Tips for Peaceful Bedtime Routines." *Next Step 4 ADHD* (blog), March 13, 2020. https://nextstep4adhd.com/5-tips-for-bedtime-adhd/.

Ahmed, Gellan K., Nabil A. Metwaly, Khaled Elbeh, Marwa Salah Galal, and Islam Shaaban. "Prevalence of School Bullying and Its Relationship with Attention Deficit-Hyperactivity Disorder and Conduct Disorder: A Cross-Sectional Study." *The Egyptian Journal of Neurology, Psychiatry and Neurosurgery* 58, no. 1 (2022): 60. https://doi.org/10.1186/s41983-022-00494-6.

Becker, Stephen P. "ADHD and Sleep: Recent Advances and Future Directions." *Current Opinion in Psychology* 34 (August 2020): 50–56. https://doi.org/10.1016/j.copsyc.2019.09.006.

"Blocking Out Noise: Reduce Distractions for ADHD Brains." https://www.additudemag.com/9-tips-for-blocking-out-noise/.

Buzanko, Dr Caroline. "How to Manage Impulsive Behaviours in Kids with ADHD." *Dr. Caroline Buzanko* (blog), September 27, 2019. https://drcarolinebuzanko.com/how-to-manage-impulsive-behaviours-in-kids-with-adhd/.

Carney, Amy Giguere. "Self-Care Strategies for Parents & Caregivers." https://medicine.yale.edu/news-article/self-care-strategies-parents/.

CDC. "ADHD in the Classroom: Helping Children Succeed in School." Attention-Deficit / Hyperactivity Disorder (ADHD), July 25, 2024. https://www.cdc.gov/adhd/treatment/classroom.html.

"Diagnosing ADHD." Attention-Deficit / Hyperactivity Disorder (ADHD), May 15, 2024. https://www.cdc.gov/adhd/diagnosis/index.html.

CHADD. "Home-School Collaboration: It's Important for Children with ADHD." https://chadd.org/attention-article/home-school-collaboration-its-important-for-children-with-adhd/.

REFERENCES

CHADD. "Parenting a Child with ADHD." https://chadd.org/for-parents/overview/.

Child Mind Institute. "ADHD and Exercise." https://childmind.org/article/adhd-and-exercise/.

Day, Nicole. "Mindfulness for ADHD: Benefits and Activities for Kids." *Raising An Extraordinary Person* (blog), November 17, 2017. https://hes-extraordinary.com/manage-adhd-mindfulness.

"Deep Breathing for the ADHD Brain." https://www.additudemag.com/deep-breathing-exercises-for-adhd-meditation/.

Derbyshire, E. "Do Omega-3/6 Fatty Acids Have a Therapeutic Role in Children and Young People with ADHD?" *Journal of Lipids* 2017 (2017): 6285218. https://doi.org/10.1155/2017/6285218.

"DESR and ADHD: The Overlooked Emotional Component of ADHD." https://www.additudemag.com/desr-adhd-emotional-regulation/.

"Emotional Regulation in ADHD Children: How to Teach Control." https://www.additudemag.com/emotional-regulation-skills-adhd-children/.

Fang, Yuan, Jing Liu, Borui Zhang, Man Lau, Ying Fung Ho, Yaxi Yang, Yan Shi, Eric Tsz Chun Poon, Andy Choi Yeung Tse, and Fenghua Sun. "A Systematic Review of the Benefits and Mechanisms of Family-Based Mind-Body Therapy Programs Targeting Families of Children and Adolescents with Attention-Deficit/Hyperactivity Disorder." *Journal of Social and Personal Relationships* 41, no. 8 (August 2024): 2219–50. https://doi.org/10.1177/02654075241239878.

Flynn, Lori. "Effective Visual Schedules for ADHD." OT4ADHD, August 8, 2022. https://ot4adhd.com/2022/08/08/effective-visual-schedules-for-adhd/.

Frida. "ADHD Meltdowns: What Causes Them and How to Minimize Their Impact." https://www.talkwithfrida.com/learn/adhd-meltdowns-causes-tips-strategies/.

Goally. "ADHD and Social Cues in Kids." *Goally Apps & Tablets for Kids* (blog), October 30, 2023. https://getgoally.com/blog/adhd-and-social-cues-in-kids/.

"Do Visual Schedules Help ADHD Students?" *Goally Apps & Tablets for Kids* (blog), February 7, 2024. https://getgoally.com/blog/do-visual-schedules-help-adhd-students/.

Healthline. "7 Ways to Calm Your Child with ADHD," March 26, 2018. https://www.healthline.com/health/adhd/calm-children-natural-remedies.

Healthline. "Types of ADHD: Inattentive, Hyperactive-Impulsive, and More," June 19, 2013. https://www.healthline.com/health/adhd/three-types-adhd.

"How to Celebrate Your Teen's ADHD." https://parents.au.reachout.com/mental-health-and-wellbeing/adhd/celebrating-adhd.

"How to Get an IEP or 504 Plan for ADHD in 8 Steps." https://www.additudemag.com/504-plan-for-adhd-accommodations-at-school/.

Huntington Learning Center. "Creating Home Behavior Charts That Actually

Work!," October 4, 2021. https://huntingtonhelps.com/resources/adhd-blog/creating-home-behavior-charts

Lange, Klaus W., Susanne Reichl, Katharina M. Lange, Lara Tucha, and Oliver Tucha. "The History of Attention Deficit Hyperactivity Disorder." *Attention Deficit and Hyperactivity Disorders* 2, no. 4 (2010): 241–55. https://doi.org/10.1007/s12402-010-0045-8.

"Life Skills: Your ADHD Teen Can Build Independence & Confidence." https://www.additudemag.com/life-skills-adhd-kids-need-to-know/.

Masters, Tom. "Clutter, Stress and ADHD." Edge Foundation, February 17, 2023. https://edgefoundation.org/clutter-stress-and-adhd/.

Mautone, Jennifer A., Elizabeth K. Lefler, and Thomas J. Power. "Promoting Family and School Success for Children With ADHD: Strengthening Relationships While Building Skills." *Theory into Practice* 50, no. 1 (2011): 43–51. https://doi.org/10.1080/00405841.2010.534937.

McArthur, Keith. "4 Strategies for Planning Family Outings When Your Kid Has ADHD." Today's Parent, October 15, 2021. https://www.todaysparent.com/family/special-needs/strategies-for-planning-family-outings-when-your-kid-has-adhd/.

Mehrabian, A. (1970). Measures of vocabulary and grammatical skills for children up to age six. Developmental Psychology, 2, 439-446.

"Morning Routine for Families: Get to Work & School On Time." https://www.additudemag.com/adhd-morning-routine-stress-free-kids/.

Neuropsychology, Pathways. "Positive Reinforcement in Children and Adolescents with ADHD - Psychologists | Toms River, Manahawkin, Freehold, NJ." *Pathways Neuropsychology Associates* (blog), February 2, 2021. https://www.pathwaysneuropsychology.com/positive-reinforcement-in-children-and-adolescents-with-adhd/.

PhD, Ellen Braaten. "How to Prepare for a Parent-Teacher Conference If Your Child Has ADHD." Clay Center for Young Healthy Minds, September 11, 2019. https://www.mghclaycenter.org/parenting-concerns/grade-school/how-to-prepare-for-parent-teacher-conference-if-child-has-adhd/.

Pinto, Sofia, Teresa Correia-de-Sá, Benedita Sampaio-Maia, Carla Vasconcelos, Pedro Moreira, and Joana Ferreira-Gomes. "Eating Patterns and Dietary Interventions in ADHD: A Narrative Review." *Nutrients* 14, no. 20 (October 16, 2022): 4332. https://doi.org/10.3390/nu14204332.

Rich, Erika Carpenter, Sandra K. Loo, May Yang, Jeff Dang, and Susan L. Smalley. "Social Functioning Difficulties in ADHD: Association with PDD Risk." *Clinical Child Psychology and Psychiatry* 14, no. 3 (July 2009): 329–44. https://doi.org/10.1177/1359104508100890.

Schreier, Janice. "Helping a Child with ADHD Develop Social Skills." Mayo Clinic Health System, n.d. https://www.mayoclinichealthsystem.org/home

town-health/speaking-of-health/helping-a-child-with-adhd-develop-social-skills.

Setyanisa, Alma Rossabela, Yunias Setiawati, Irwanto Irwanto, Izzatul Fithriyah, and Satria Arief Prabowo. "Relationship between Parenting Style and Risk of Attention Deficit Hyperactivity Disorder in Elementary School Children." *The Malaysian Journal of Medical Sciences: MJMS* 29, no. 4 (August 2022): 152–59. https://doi.org/10.21315/mjms2022.29.4.14.

Skogli, Erik Winther, Martin H Teicher, Per Normann Andersen, Kjell Tore Hovik, and Merete Øie. "ADHD in Girls and Boys – Gender Differences in Co-Existing Symptoms and Executive Function Measures." *BMC Psychiatry* 13 (November 9, 2013): 298. https://doi.org/10.1186/1471-244X-13-298.

"Social Skills Role Play: Friendship Tips for Kids with ADHD." https://www.additudemag.com/building-social-skills/.

Storebø, Ole Jakob, Mette Elmose Andersen, Maria Skoog, Signe Joost Hansen, Erik Simonsen, Nadia Pedersen, Britta Tendal, Henriette E. Callesen, Erlend Faltinsen, and Christian Gluud. "Social Skills Training for Attention Deficit Hyperactivity Disorder (ADHD) in Children Aged 5 to 18 Years." *The Cochrane Database of Systematic Reviews* 2019, no. 6 (June 21, 2019): CD008223. https://doi.org/10.1002/14651858.CD008223.pub3.

"Strengths-Based Teaching for ADHD Students." https://www.additudemag.com/strengths-based-teaching/.

True Reflections Mental Health Services. "Communication Strategies for Parents of ADHD Kids." https://www.truereflectionsmhs.com/blog/communication-parents-adhd-kids.

Urbanowicz, Agata Maria, Rebecca Shankland, Jaynie Rance, Paul Bennett, Christophe Leys, and Aurélie Gauchet. "Cognitive Behavioral Stress Management for Parents: Prevention and Reduction of Parental Burnout." *International Journal of Clinical and Health Psychology: IJCHP* 23, no. 4 (2023): 100365. https://doi.org/10.1016/j.ijchp.2023.100365.

Verywell Mind. "How to Find an ADHD Support Group." https://www.verywellmind.com/how-to-find-an-adhd-support-group-5324827.

"What Is Self-Awareness? How to Teach Self-Advocacy Skills to ADHD Kids." https://www.additudemag.com/self-awareness-activities-self-advocacy-skills-adhd/.

Wilens, Dr. Timothy. "ADHD in Teens: How Symptoms Manifest as Unique Challenges for Adolescents and Young Adults." ADDitude, n.d. https://www.additudemag.com/adhd-in-teens-challenges-solutions/.

Xu, Guifeng, Lane Strathearn, Buyun Liu, Binrang Yang, and Wei Bao. "Twenty-Year Trends in Diagnosed Attention-Deficit/Hyperactivity Disorder Among US Children and Adolescents, 1997-2016." *JAMA Network Open* 1, no. 4 (August 31, 2018): e181471. https://doi.org/10.1001/jamanetworkopen.2018.1471.

Printed in Dunstable, United Kingdom